The School-Choice Controversy

The School-Choice Controversy

What Is Constitutional?

Edited by **James W. Skillen**

The Center for Public Justice
Washington, DC 20002

Baker Books

A Division of Baker Book House Co
Grand Rapids, Michigan 49516

© 1993 by The Center for Public Justice

Published by Baker Books
a division of Baker Book House Company
P.O. Box 6287, Grand Rapids, Michigan 49516-6287

Printed in the United States of America

Library of Congress Cataloging-in-Publication Data

The school choice controversy : what is constitutional? / edited by James W.
Skillen.
    p.   cm.
Includes bibliographical references and index.
ISBN 0-8010-8361-3
    1. School, Choice of—United States. 2. School, Choice of—Law and
legislation—United States. 3. Educational vouchers—United States. 4. School,
Choice of—Social aspects—United States. 5. Church and state—United States.
6. Public schools—United States. I. Skillen, James W.
LB1027.9.S353 1993
371'.01—dc20   93-29461

Chapter 1 © by Richard A. Baer, Jr., and used by permission.

Contents

Introduction

"School choice" has jumped out into the open. The topic is hot. American education cries out for reform, and choice seems to be one of the answers. But what is the question? What does choice mean? What is it supposed to do? And does the Constitution permit it?

Business leaders wonder how their companies will be able to compete in the global marketplace if their employees are not better educated. Many believe that choice can help by forcing schools to adapt to the disciplines of a competitive market.

Politicians struggle to justify increased public expenditures. Some believe that granting a measure of choice to parents can help restore public confidence in both schools and government, thereby building support for the taxes that are necessary to sustain and improve education.

Parents worry about the moral as well as the economic future of their children. Some believe that choice among government-run schools can help them find the best place for their children within the current system. Other parents, however, prefer nongovernment schools or home schooling, and some of them would like to receive greater public financial support for their efforts.

Many independent schools believe that they deserve some if not all of the support given to public schools. Other independent schools, however, want nothing to do with government aid or entanglement. Nongovernment schools offer parents an alternative to the public system, and they don't want government to intrude.

Can school choice satisfy all of these needs and desires? What about the dangers and problems that might come with opening the existing system to choice, or of going even further and allowing parents to choose nongovernment schools as well? Will choice destroy the long-established pattern that has helped create the great American melting pot? Will it aggravate racial discrimination and segregation? And if tax-supported choice ever extends beyond the government-controlled sector, will it violate the separation of church and state?

These and many other questions arise as soon as the subject of school choice comes up. They are important questions, urgent questions. We need to face them squarely. They are especially critical for people with strong religious convictions who stand on different sides of the school-choice issue. Education is connected with the deepest aspirations we have for our children's future. It is wrapped up with questions about truth and falsehood, about right and wrong, about God and country. Schooling inevitably touches life's deepest meaning and purpose. It concerns the most intimate as well as the most public responsibilities people bear. Will greater freedom for school choice promote or restrict the American quest both to respect religious freedom and diversity as well as to knit citizens together in a common civic order of justice for all?

This book focuses on one of the most fundamental challenges facing the school-choice movement, namely, that of the Constitution's mandates and restrictions. No matter what the consequences might be for the economy, for race relations, for class distinctions, or for civic training, the foremost question about choice in the American system is a constitutional one.

In November 1991 a remarkable symposium was held on this topic in Tacoma, Washington, jointly sponsored by the University of Puget Sound Law School and the Washington Federation of Independent Schools. The four principal speakers at that conference are the contributors to this book. While the symposium gave special attention to the situation in the state of Washington, the issues under consideration are national in scope. Moreover, the speakers—from California, New York, Georgia, and Washington, D.C.— have been engaged in the debate on this subject in all parts of the country for many years.

Therefore, with encouragement from the symposium's organizer, Carl T. Fynboe, the Center for Public Justice asked the speakers to revise their papers for publication. The center has, from its inception, argued for the reform of American public education to allow for greater pluralism and to enhance parental responsibility. The center's concern has always been both for the public good and for families, both for a healthier political community and for diverse schools. It is the hope of both the authors and the center that this book will help take the debate over school choice beyond political slogans and interest-group combat to serious public discussion.

In the opening essay, Richard Baer argues that the very idea of a "strict and lofty neutrality as to religion" is an unachievable goal within a monopoly public school system. The real constitutional question, says Baer, is not whether religious schools can pass a First Amendment test but whether the present public school system can pass that test. The answer, he concludes, is No. For government to act with fairness and equity in schooling, it should give parents vouchers to use in the schools of their choice—whether religious or secular.

Attorney and history professor Edward Larson analyzes the implications of the so-called Blaine amendment, which dates back to the late nineteenth century and is named after its chief promoter, Rep. James G. Blaine. That amendment, which can be found in many state constitutions, prohibits government aid to all "sectarian" activities including religious schools. The *Witters* case in the State of Washington, which reached the U.S. Supreme Court in 1986, well illustrates the constitutional questions at stake here. Larson tries to show what would have to transpire if a state that sticks with current interpretations of the Blaine amendment were to decide to fund school choice outside of its state-run system of common schools.

Berkeley law professor Phillip Johnson takes a different approach to the *Witters* case. He argues for changes in legal reasoning that are necessary to get the courts to *reinterpret* the First Amendment to the U.S. Constitution. Parents, says Johnson, should be free to choose either religious or secular education for their children on equivalent financial terms, because there is nothing religiously neutral about so-called secular education. Religious freedom in accord with the First Amendment should mean equal treatment for all citizens in their choice of schools.

Finally, James Skillen draws together many strands of the earlier arguments to contend for a new and coherent philosophy of educational pluralism. Government's job is to do justice—to parents, to children, to teachers, to schools, to religious convictions, and to all citizens who share the same public space and civic life. Government should not turn its back on schooling and let the chips fall where they may by simply privatizing education. Rather, it should do justice to every citizen by allowing fair and equitable choice among different school systems, none of which has to be owned and operated by government.

To some readers the arguments in the following chapters may sound new and far too radical. But, for the most part, that reaction arises from a lack of familiarity with the arguments, some of which have been around for a long time. When the U.S. Supreme Court first began to rule on cases dealing with the relation of religion to public schooling back in the 1940s (*Everson* v. *Board of Education* [1947] and *McCollum* v. *Board of Education* [1948]), one of the astute critics at the time posed many of the questions that we pursue in this book. In an address in 1948, Catholic scholar John Courtney Murray commented that the public school, as defined by the Court, had reached a point of self-contradiction: "It exists, supposedly, in order to promote democracy. Yet it is constitutionally forbidden to promote those religious beliefs which are the foundation of democracy."[1]

In the "philosophy of education" articulated by some of the Supreme Court justices in the 1940s Murray found little room "for the rights of the parent over the child" and "for the subjection of government itself to the wishes of the parent." He viewed "with intense alarm the development of a philosophy of public education in which the principle of separation of church and state would somehow entail, as a consequence, the separation of the parent from the child."[2]

Murray also began to expose a problem that Richard Baer confronts so directly in his essay, namely, the religious character of what might at first appear to be a nonreligious faith in democracy. "This 'religion of democracy' is our great contemporary myth," said Murray.

It is a secularist system of values, constructed without reference
to God or to any human destiny beyond this world, that presents
itself as a higher, more unifying religion than all "sectarianism."
It looks down with contempt upon the rivalries of sects, as somehow un-American. It wants all sectarian religion kept out of the
public school, as divisive of the mystical unity of the American
people, at the same time that it asserts itself to be the proper object
of government support and promotion. Someone has called this
'religion of democracy' the 'public school sect.' It is truly a sectarian religion, with an orthodoxy and a vocabulary all its own.[3]

During the past forty-five years, the Supreme Court has
not managed to resolve the ambiguities and contradictions
inherent in its many rulings in this area. But the Court does
not stand isolated in its predicament. We, the American people, find ourselves in the same boat. We are uncertain about,
and divided over, government's proper role in dealing with
religion and education.

It is our hope that this book will help many take a step
forward to an intellectually sound and politically peaceful
resolution of one of America's oldest conflicts. The arguments may be strong and radical, but the time has come for
constitutional clarity and integrity.

Contributors

Richard A. Baer, Jr. is Professor of Environmental Ethics at Cornell University and a Fellow of the Center for Public Justice. He earned his Ph.D. at Harvard University. His essays have appeared in scientific, philosophical, and theological journals, and his op-ed pieces have appeared in the *Wall Street Journal, Education Week,* and other popular media.

Phillip E. Johnson is Jefferson E. Peyser Professor of Law at the University of California, Berkeley. His J.D. degree is from the University of Chicago. He is the author of *Darwin on Trial* (1991) and of numerous journal articles on constitutional and criminal law, philosophy of science, and religion.

Edward J. Larson is Associate Professor of History and Law at the University of Georgia. He holds the Ph.D. from the University of Wisconsin in the history of science and the J.D. from Harvard Law School. He is the author of *Trial and Error: The American Controversy over Creation and Evolution* (1989) and of a forthcoming book on eugenics in the deep South.

James W. Skillen is Executive Director of the Center for Public Justice. He earned his Ph.D. in political science at Duke University. He is the author of *The Scattered Voice: Christians at Odds in the Public Square* (1990) and the editor (with Rockne McCarthy) of *Political Order and the Plural Structure of Society* (1991). He edits the Center's PUBLIC JUSTICE REPORT and writes regularly for other journals and magazines on both international and domestic affairs.

"Strict Neutrality" and Our Monopoly System

Richard A. Baer, Jr.

Every curriculum that is more than simple technical instruction in, say, how to operate a computer or drive a car (and even these are not true exceptions) rests on fundamental understandings and commitments regarding the nature of reality itself, the nature of the good life and the good society, and how one ought to live. These commitments are not neutral for various religious claimants, nor are they neutral for religious claimants as over against secular philosophical claimants. Let me be more specific. Whenever either secular education or religious education deals with what I call

15

the "Big Questions"—Who are we? What is reality like? How ought we to live? What is worthy of our deepest loyalty and commitment?—it will not be neutral in terms of religion and nonreligion. There are no neutral answers to the Big Questions.

On the other hand, if education attempts to avoid taking a stand on such issues altogether, it will be, at best, random and chaotic. Any consistent educational vision, any coherent curriculum, and any effective approach to help students develop integrity and character as well as to gain particular bits of knowledge and technical competence in various skills depends on specific views of the nature of reality and of the good life. And whatever educators may say to the contrary, the social reality in America today is that we have become a radically pluralistic society. There is no longer basic agreement on the nature of the good life or on the goals, content, and appropriate methods of education.

It is easiest to appreciate this point in relation to courses in government public schools that deal with values, sex education, human relations, decision making, and other matters having to do with how we ought to live.[1] Take the example of Values Clarification, a method for teaching values that became popular in many schools roughly twenty years ago. The method was widely advertised as value-neutral. Teachers were not to indoctrinate students with their values and moral commitments, but were to assist students in the clarification of their own "personal values." Various exercises and strategies employed by Values Clarification proved popular with students and teachers alike, and the movement spread like wildfire through school systems across the nation.[2]

Some parents, however, were not impressed with either the method or its results, and during the 1970s and early 1980s schools were torn with constant strife over its use.

Scholars and even groups of laypeople gradually produced an extensive and, in some cases, highly sophisticated literature extremely critical of the method. They concluded that Values Clarification was by no means value-neutral as claimed. For instance, the method simply assumed, without offering any justification, that all value judgments (including moral claims) were purely subjective matters of mere personal opinion and preference. According to Values Clarification, no one could legitimately say that one set of values was better than any other. Thus, understandably, teachers should limit their role to clarifying the student's own values and never presume to teach any values as "correct" or "true."

But, of course, it is by no means self-evident that all value or moral claims are purely subjective; indeed few first-rate philosophical or theological ethicists today are subjectivists or radical relativists. But more pertinent to our concerns here is the fact that this claim directly competed with and undermined the claims of Christians, Jews, and adherents of other religions who believe that values, particularly moral values, are not mainly matters of subjective preference.

Similarly, with no proffered justification and without acknowledging that many reasonable people and most of the world's great religions strongly disagree, Values Clarification simply assumed a hedonistic view of life—that the meaning and purpose of life are self-fulfillment, meeting one's own needs, and satisfying one's own desires. But what possible right, we must ask, did the state have to indoctrinate (I use the term carefully and deliberately) children in this belief, particularly in light of the fact that it directly competed with and undermined what their parents wanted them to learn about these matters? Most Jews and Christians clearly cannot accept such a self-centered, individualistic view of what life is all about. Christian and Jewish parents, at least if they take their faith seriously, believe that they should teach their children to love God, seek justice, and serve their neighbor—goals far removed from the narcissistic hedonism of Values Clarification.

It gradually became clear to parents and other critics that Values Clarification might well cause students to defect from the beliefs that their parents and churches were teaching them. Teachers, as agents of the state, were employing a method of teaching values that gave what was, in effect, establishment status to particular beliefs about the nature of morality and the good life, beliefs that are highly offensive to many traditionally religious people—as well as to many nontheistic humanists who are neither subjectivists nor egoistic hedonists. Furthermore, by undermining the beliefs and values that many parents and churches teach children—beliefs and values that are part of the core convictions of religions like Christianity and Judaism—the state was not only establishing its own "religion" but also hindering the free exercise of religion of those who believe differently. From an ethical or philosophical standpoint, a strong case can be made that government public schools regularly violate both parts of the religion clause of the First Amendment.[3]

Unfortunately, many school administrators and teachers (not to mention those who developed Values Clarification) tried to portray the objections of parents opposed to the method as the anti-intellectual ranting of right-wing fundamentalists and religious fanatics who wanted to "censor" the free exchange of ideas in public schools. And the authors of the method—Sidney Simon, Howard Kirschenbaum, and others—never seriously responded to their critics, who included first-rate philosophers, theologians, and ethicists at America's top universities,[4] preferring instead to direct ad hominem arguments against the critics.[5] But even more frustrating than such personal attacks was the fact that proponents of Values Clarification almost totally ignored scholarly criticisms of the method. The entire episode represents a shabby chapter in American educational and intellectual history.[6]

Over the past twenty years parents and academics have leveled almost identical complaints against a variety of sex education curricula and home economics texts that have been used in government public school systems across the nation. These curricula typically pressed upon students highly subjectivist approaches to morality; assumed a hedonistic view of life; tended to undermine the authority of tradition, family, and church; and presented human relations in terms of a kind of cost-benefit analysis.[7] Such curricular materials directly conflicted with the teachings of traditional religions. In many cases authors of these materials presented their own ideas as more rational or more scientific than those the students were learning from family and church. They were up-to-date ideas, based on the work of specialists and experts, not on convention or tradition.[8]

When parents and others criticized these materials, the educational establishment—particularly the National Education Association—typically took a defensive posture. And the popular media tended uncritically to accept the educational establishment's interpretations of these conflicts with parents and church groups. As in the case of Values Clarification, professional educators refused to take their critics seriously on an academic level and instead focused on how to outwit and overpower them politically. Because some of the protesting parents were not academically sophisticated, they were vulnerable to the charge that they were simply uneducated fundamentalists who were not quite ready to embrace modern science and accept the reality of the twentieth century.

My best professional judgment, however, is that many of these relatively uneducated parents were more thoughtful and philosophically sophisticated in their criticisms of various sex education curricula and home economics texts than were the authors of these materials, the teachers and school administrators who used them, and representatives of the popular media who reported on the conflicts engendered by their use. Virtually all of my direct experience of such conflicts makes me confident of this claim. Indeed it is amazing how often parents anticipated the objections to such material raised by first-rate scholars at some of our best universities.

Even if my analysis is correct, would it not be possible for schools to remove the bias from these materials? Such a suggestion is not without merit. Although Values Clarification is so fundamentally biased that trying to reform it would in effect destroy it, sex education curricula could be made a good deal fairer and less objectionable.

But the issue of religious neutrality would still remain unresolved. For one thing, it is no simple task in a highly pluralistic society to state clearly what neutrality would consist of in matters like sex education. But even if these materials were altogether eliminated from the curriculum, there is a more basic issue at stake, namely that *the entire curriculum* of a school—not just these "add-ons"—is based on fundamental understandings and commitments in regard to the nature of reality and the good life. For instance, on what basis does a school decide that it is more important to emphasize math and science than, say, poetry and music? Or how should the school accommodate those parents who wish their children to learn to be less competitive, less oriented toward the consumption of natural resources and the exploitation of nature? A curriculum that prepares students for economic success in the world of technology, industry, and high finance is certainly not neutral for the children of these parents. Or what do government schools have to say to parents who believe that fundamental to all education is the goal of learning to love God and serve one's fellow human beings? With respect to families who embrace such a belief how can one possibly pretend that our present schools are religiously neutral?

Classical liberals typically recommend that schools emphasize diversity, exposing students to a variety of moral and religious views and then encouraging them to choose for themselves which to accept. Keep the marketplace of ideas open, and students will be free to exercise their autonomy and realize their true identity as they choose among various contending positions. This approach, the liberal claims, will safeguard children from the potential moral, religious, and cognitive tyranny of parents. It will prevent the family from totally dominating the values and thinking of the child, thus respecting the autonomy of children and fostering their growth toward maturity and independence. And, perhaps most important of all, it will help achieve one of the primary goals of a liberal education: to make children more tolerant of people who are different from themselves.[9]

But at least five objections can be raised against the marketplace-of-ideas approach to public education.

First, we have no reliable empirical evidence that such a method actually makes children more tolerant of other people. Instead, it may simply leave them vulnerable to the next demagogue who appears on the scene offering them definite (and almost certainly simplistic) answers to life's tough questions and demanding that they make firm commitments to the demagogue's ideology.

Second, the best the marketplace approach can do is give students a smattering of knowledge about the major contenders in the cultural marketplace. In a society as diverse as our own, most minority positions simply will not be reflected in the school curriculum. This, I think, is one of the valid points (one of the very few valid points!) of the multiculturalists who are clamoring for more control over the curriculum in public schools. No school curriculum can remain coherent and do justice to the truly incredible range of cultural, religious, and moral diversity of our society today.

Third, a far more serious objection is the fact that the marketplace view of the school curriculum rests on a fundamentally flawed assumption about the nature of human freedom and choice. It simply is not the case that students in our primary and secondary schools are in a position to make intelligent, informed choices from among competing values and worldviews on the basis of the very meager understanding of these positions presented to them in a government public school. Not only is there not enough time to do justice to the complexity of various traditions, but by limiting understanding of different traditions mainly to what can be conveyed with words, students will fail to experience what can be conveyed only by actual participation in the overall life of a particular community. It is also this more complete experience that is essential for the development of character.

Fourth, the marketplace-of-ideas approach always carries with it an implied relativism that is anything but religiously or ethically neutral. We would never consider teaching science in such a manner. Why should we do so in ethics and religion?

Finally, the marketplace-of-ideas model demands that teachers present diverse ideas, values, and religious beliefs fairly and objectively, but this is an impossible requirement within the government public school. The Supreme Court leaves open the door for the study "of" religion in public schools so long as it is done "objectively."[10] But how is this possible? Should the Bible be taught as part of a course in history or English literature?[11] Would such an approach be religiously neutral or more objective or fairer than to study the Bible as Scripture? Christians have always held that the Bible is Scripture and have treated it as Scripture. For them to read the Bible merely as literature is to distort it and to misconstrue its significance for their lives. What the Court fails to realize is that its assumption that the Bible can be taught objectively or as literature is a *particular* assumption compatible with a liberal, Enlightenment worldview. Scholars who accept a comparative religion approach to sacred texts may feel at home with it. But it is not an acceptable approach for most committed Christians, and those who think at all deeply about the matter will realize that it is quite unacceptable to consider such an approach "objective."

Inasmuch as values are imparted not just through formal studies but also through the total ambience of a school, it seems clear to me that even if a religiously neutral curriculum were achievable it would not result in a religiously neutral school. For better or worse, teachers and administrators inevitably function as role models for children. Government public schools have often tried to make a sharp distinction between the public professional qualifications and the private lives of teachers when it comes to hiring and promotion. But it is not at all obvious that this separation works well when it comes to teaching values. For one thing, it conveys to students the by no means neutral belief that life can be effectively compartmentalized—that who we are in one area of our lives does not significantly affect who we are in other areas. Also, the fact that public schools feel constrained to treat the teacher simply as a professional rather than as a total human being (as many independent religious schools try to do) greatly limits the degree to which teachers can be significant role models. They can model certain academic virtues, but the state can insist on little beyond this as a requirement for employment.

In a Christian school, students can learn the important lesson that faith in God and in Jesus Christ significantly affects how one views the world in its totality. One's religious life and one's academic life are not separated into two watertight compartments, but are integrated. This is not a religiously neutral position, but it is not obviously less neutral than the isolation of the two realms from each other.

Consider another contrast between a government public school and an independent school. In a Christian school, classes may be opened with prayer, or a prayer may be spoken before lunch or at the beginning of a school assembly. Also, the school is free to hold a religious baccalaureate service for students at the time of graduation. All of this is problematic in a government school. But is it religiously neutral to exclude prayer from government public schools? Of course it is not. Not to pray is no more neutral than to pray. One possible compromise that would move the government public school closer to neutrality would be to institute a moment of silence at the beginning of each class or before meals or school assemblies, during which students could either pray or use the silence for quiet personal reflection or meditation.[12] But strong church-state separationists are not interested in such compromises. Their demand is that the school become totally secular—all under the illusion that it will thereby become religiously neutral. Strict separationists either do not realize or else deliberately deemphasize the fact that such a commitment gives a de facto establishment status to secularized views of education, the nature of human beings, and the good society. And a secularized worldview *functions* like any religious view.

The Historical Rootedness of All Human Thinking

The truth is that all human thinking about the nature of reality and all large-scale worldviews, theologies, or philosophies, are dependent on initial commitments or assumptions that are not necessarily unreasonable, but cannot be proven by reason as such. It is not just theological thinkers who make such assumptions. Humanists, atheists, and Marxists all do the same. There are no good philosophical grounds for believing that secular thinking about the nature of the good life and the good society is reasonable in a sense that is fundamentally different from the reasonableness of Christian or Jewish thinking.[13]

All human thinking starts with certain commitments and assumptions. All human thinking entails the risk of error. Even though I as a Christian believe that the Christian gospel is true in a unique sense, I have to admit the fact that I may be wrong. And exactly the same is true of the follower of Jeremy Bentham, of Karl Marx, of John Dewey, or of John Rawls. The framers of *Humanist Manifestos I* and *II* may honestly believe that they are reasonable in some unique sense, but the truth of their belief is by no means obvious to Christians or Marxists or even to humanists of differing persuasions. Recent developments in epistemology simply do not support the claim that secular thinkers are in possession of a completely rational, scientific algorithm that will give assured results in history, literary criticism, religious studies, and ethics as well as in the natural sciences.[14]

In any case, whether you and I believe we possess the truth in some unique sense, government within the American political tradition is acting illegitimately when it makes such a claim about matters having to do with the Big Questions—questions about the meaning and purpose of human existence. Whenever government uses the term "nonsectarian" to refer to the realm of the secular and the term "sectarian" to refer to the realm of the religious, it is out of order. Nor will it do to claim that the term "sectarian" has now been used for such a long time as a synonym for "religious" that it has lost its pejorative, discriminatory meaning. First, that claim is empirically false. The term carries with it so many of its older pejorative connotations that it remains demonstrably discriminatory in its impact on thinking about contemporary legal and philosophical issues having to do with religion and public life, including education.[15] Second, the disturbing history of the meaning of the term mandates that government stop using it even if only out of simple respect for religious Americans. Its continued usage clouds discussion of issues vitally important to civil peace and justice in our common life.

The truth is that when it comes to the realm of education and the Big Questions the secular domain is just as parochial, limited, and "sectarian" as is the religious domain. Dewey as a secular thinker is not obviously less provincial than theologian Karl Barth or Reinhold Niebuhr. Even if this claim were not true, in our political system it would never be appropriate for *government* to say otherwise.

As American we long ago learned that it is possible for us to do much of our ordinary public business without emphasizing our particular religious or denominational differences. This was an important discovery. Indeed, it is hard to believe that there is a distinctive Presbyterian method for dredging harbors, a special Jewish technique for running a post office, or a superior Roman Catholic method for provisioning the military. In these "secular" spheres, including most areas of our ordinary economic activity, we discovered early in our history that we could get along with each other more peaceably if we downplayed our religious and theological (that is, our denominational) differences. No quarrel so far.

But when it comes to the domain of education and the Big Questions, we face an entirely different situation. It makes perfectly good sense to think of a Catholic view of divorce, an Orthodox Jewish perspective on the family, or an evangelical Protestant understanding of abortion. When it comes to questions about the meaning and purpose of life—and what curriculum does not rest on judgments, even if only implicit, about these matters?—it makes no sense to argue that secular thinking is neutral in a way that religious thinking is not. If government can act only in a secular fashion in education, then it is imperative for government to get out of the business of actually operating public schools altogether, for secular answers to the Big Questions never are religiously neutral. They violate the spirit of the First Amendment just as clearly as do religious answers. It is absurd to think that it is religiously neutral to teach students that the meaning and purpose of life is to pursue pleasure by satisfying one's own needs and desires. Such "secular" doctrines are at least as "sectarian" as the conviction that the purpose of life is to glorify God and to serve the needs of one's neighbors.[16]

Actually, both Jefferson and Horace Mann—and this was true of most Americans until late in the nineteenth century—simply assumed that proper education would include instruction in morality and religion. The presidents of virtually all of our major colleges and universities until the late nineteenth century were clergymen. Religious and moral instruction was almost universally required of college students. Education was seen as religious through and through. When educators extolled the value of "nonsectarian" education most of them were thinking of education that was "nondenominational," not education that was purely secular.

That most Americans assumed a close relationship between education and religion may indeed help to explain why John Dewey and other early nontheistic humanists referred to their own thinking as religious or sometimes as constituting a new religion. They understood that education did not take place in a philosophical or theological vacuum, and they also knew that, although there was strong opposition to "sectarian" (in the sense of denominational) education, there was much support for the close association of education with religion. The closing words of Dewey's book *A Common Faith* claim: "Here are all the elements for a religious faith that shall not be confined to sect, class, or race. Such a faith has always been implicitly the common faith of mankind. It remains to make it explicit and militant."[17] Although Dewey's claim that his humanistic faith was always "implicitly the common faith of mankind" has little to commend it historically, his final words about making his secular, nontheistic faith "explicit and militant" were prophetic, and it is no wonder that thoughtful religious leaders reacted with alarm. Their concern was only heightened when Dewey proclaimed that by advancing a common culture America's public schools "are performing an infinitely significant religious work."[18]

Indeed, the claim that secular humanism is a religion was not originally made by Catholic and Protestant fundamentalist critics of humanism but by humanists themselves. Humanist J. H. Randall expressed the conviction that "the faith that alone promises salvation is the faith in intelligence."[19] In the preface to his book *Humanism: A New Religion*, Dr. Charles Francis Potter writes: "The purpose of this book is to set forth . . . the principal points of the new religion called Humanism."[20] Potter claims that "Humanism is not another denomination of Protestant Christianity; it is not a creed; nor is it a cult. It is a new type of religion altogether."[21]

Such claims were commonplace among nontheistic or secular humanists, and are particularly prominent in *Humanist Manifesto I* (1933), which explicitly defines humanism as religious and as constituting a new religion. The very last paragraph begins with the sentence: "So stand the theses of religious humanism."

But even *Humanist Manifesto II* (1973) uses terms like "faith" and "commitment," and refers to "the ultimate goal" of human existence, namely, "the fulfillment of the potential for growth in each human personality." "Humanism," the authors claim, "can provide the purpose and inspiration that so many seek; it can give personal meaning and significance to human life." It is a "positive belief in the possibilities of human progress." The authors boldly declare that "no deity will save us; we must save ourselves." Here, clearly, are hallmarks of religion, notably a set of beliefs that deal with human existence at its deepest (or most transcendent) level, discuss the means of salvation (science and education), and attempt to explain the place of human beings in the universe.[22]

The Need for a Functional Definition of Religion

If we are to deal justly with the relation between religion and education, we must adopt a *functional* definition of religion. If we limit ourselves to a substantive definition of religion, we can neither make sense of American history nor of the role of religion in American education today. I do not overlook the fact that most contemporary secular humanists claim that they are not religious and that humanism is not a religion. But we must note two things about this claim.

The first, and less important, is that the claim appears puzzling at best and opportunistic at worst. Puzzling, because I can find no serious discussion among nontheistic humanists as to why the earlier claim that they were religious and that humanism constituted a new religion was dropped. My own view is that the descriptor "religious" was dropped mainly for political reasons. As long as the religious qualification made it easier for secular humanists to gain access to the public square and particularly to public education, the claim was made with enthusiasm. But when, during the post-World War II period, the Supreme Court began to drive religion out of government public schools, this religious designation proved to be a distinct liability, and so it was discreetly dropped.

But a second and even stronger argument can be made for why we should continue to think of secular or nontheistic humanists as religious and their beliefs as constituting a religion. The results of not doing so are completely unacceptable. In dealing with freedom of conscience the Supreme Court has adopted a functional view of religion—in cases like *Seeger*[23] and *Welsh*[24]—to deal with conscientious objection to service in the military on the basis of one's deepest "religious" beliefs. It is my conviction that the First Amendment's significance for how we deal with religion has little to do with stained glass windows, bar mitzvahs, or baptismal services. Rather, it has to do with how religion encumbers people's consciences at the most transcendent (or very deepest) levels of their being and with the issue of how people with different beliefs about the fundamental nature of reality and of the good life can coexist peaceably. It is concerned about those beliefs and behaviors, which, if one is forced to violate, restrict, or deny, will entail the violation of one's deepest self.

If we do not adopt an essentially functional view of religion, the unacceptable result is a reductio ad absurdum that no fair-minded individual can possibly endorse. We end up with government-operated public schools in which adherents of traditional religions (Christians, Jews, Muslims, and others) are prohibited from recommending or advancing their beliefs and practices, but in which secular humanists, atheists, and others who claim not to be religious have free rein to foster *their* beliefs and practices—because these latter are not "religious" and their promotion is not prohibited by the First Amendment.[25]

My claim is that this is exactly what is happening in our government public schools. Educators have drawn on the ideas of John Dewey, Carl Rogers, Abraham Maslow, and behaviorist psychologists to indoctrinate students in particular secular and humanistic beliefs, and have seldom given anything remotely approximating equal time to competing Christian, Jewish, or other traditional religious beliefs. Such education, in my judgment, stands in violation of the spirit of the First Amendment, just as clearly as if we had continued to permit Christians to propagate the Christian gospel in government public schools. It results in an absolutely intolerable situation for those cognitive and religious minorities whose children are forced by government to become the "patients" of those experts who know what is good for other people's children and how they ought to lead their lives. Only the rich and those with access to privately subsidized independent schools are able to escape this government-sponsored "enlightenment"—an enlightenment that in many cases functions at an ethical and metaphysical level exactly like traditional religion.

Educational Choice: Vouchers

If my basic theses are correct, then Americans concerned about social justice should lend their support to policies that permit parents to choose alternative schools for their children without economic prejudice. Options would include both government and nongovernment schools, and the latter could be either religious or secular. Ideally, government should get out of the business of operating schools and universities altogether (except for specialized schools designed to impart particular technical skills, such as schools associated with the military or the training of postal workers), but politically such a move seems unlikely in the extreme.[26] In the near term, therefore, a choice system would be acceptable that would enable parents who object to the values and philosophical commitments of our present government public schools to find and pay for suitable alternatives for their children. Some kind of tuition voucher system probably is the best solution available to us at this time. If vouchers were given to families rather than to schools, a voucher system would less likely be viewed as violating the First Amendment and would make it possible to avoid direct payments to religious schools altogether.[27]

By inversely adjusting the worth of vouchers to family income levels, they could be used to increase distributive justice as well as to respect people's basic religious and moral commitments. Thus, in a region where the average cost of a seventh-grade education is $5,000 a year, vouchers for the very poor might start at $7,500 and taper off to as low as $2,500 for the affluent, thus permitting poor families to bid effectively for high-quality education. Handicapped students would also receive larger vouchers. No voucher school could discriminate on the basis of race or national origin. States could define their compelling interest in education by setting minimal requirements in reading, writing, math, American history, and civics, but they would leave the choice of subject matter and standards in areas outside the state's compelling interest to the discretion of individual schools.

Vouchers could also be used at what might be called the "campus school." A central core school, which could be operated either by government or by an independent agency, would offer most of the subjects of our present government public schools, but independent subschools would be situated close to the central school, perhaps in the same building. A student might take one or two classes a day in one of the subschools and the remaining classes in the central school. This would permit Catholics, Jews, evangelical Protestants, ecology-minded humanists, and others to teach sensitive subjects from their own particular perspectives but still have their students mix with children from different backgrounds. Students from one subschool could also enroll in courses in another subschool, if their parents so wished. To ease the transition to a choice system, government schools might continue to receive direct support for a period of up to five or ten years, but after that time they would have to compete for voucher students just as nongovernment schools would have to do. If government schools came to have excess space because of declining enrollments, they would be required to sell such space at reasonable rates to qualified nongovernment schools. Although government would specify its compelling interest in all education and thus set certain minimal standards and designate certain subject matters for all schools, further accreditation of schools—both government and nongovernment—might be sought on an optional basis through private accrediting agencies, as is presently done at the college level.

The closest that government can come to achieving public justice in the funding of education will be to fund individual students through some kind of voucher system. Parents or guardians will then be free to choose either religious or secular schools for their children. Since both religious and secular schools would have to be considered functionally religious, justice would be achieved by treating them both in an evenhanded manner. Government public schools that continue to exist under a voucher system would have to try to be as evenhanded as possible in the way they deal with various religious themes and ideas, including the religious themes and ideas of secular humanism. The only other alternative would be for government to stop funding education altogether. But such a libertarian decision seems quite unnecessary, and would have the effect of condemning millions of children either to no education or to inferior education.

The "Blaine Amendment" in State Constitutions

Edward J. Larson

Most commentators focus on federal constitutional barriers to school-choice programs that provide government aid for parochial school students. As Phillip Johnson's essay will demonstrate, however, those barriers have diminished as the United States Supreme Court has lowered the wall of separation between church and state over the past decade. In many areas of the law, the relaxing of federal constitutional restrictions by the Rehnquist Court has been offset somewhat by renewed attention to state constitutional restrictions on the part of some state supreme courts. At least with respect to government aid for parochial school students, this renewed attention at the state level should be accepted not only by liberals concerned with the separation of church and state but also by conservative supporters of an originalist interpretation of constitutional documents.

The federal government simply was not involved in public education during the early years of our Republic. Therefore, it is problematic to gauge the founders' intentions about government aid to parochial schools under the federal Constitution's establishment clause. It is quite likely that the founders did not consider the issue, especially since the establishment clause then applied only to federal government action.

In contrast, the drafters of many state constitutions probably had government support for parochial schools in the forefront of their minds when they composed their state establishment clauses. State and local funds have supported education since colonial times, and fierce disputes over using tax money for parochial schools predated most current state constitutions. Indeed, the disputes are as old as the common school movement, which arose during the previous century as a means of assimilating the increasingly diverse immigrant groups then entering the United States in steadily multiplying numbers. Prior to this movement, schooling took place in private or religious institutions. In contrast, the nineteenth-century common school offered what most considered to be nonsectarian, public elementary education to all local school-age children regardless of their economic class or religious belief.

The new common schools were not devoid of religious influences, however. For example, one of the most prominent early leaders of this movement was Horace Mann, secretary of the Massachusetts Board of Education from 1837 to 1849. Mann was strenuously opposed to sectarian instruction in common schools but not to instruction that promoted religiously based moral values. He summarized this view in his final annual report to the Massachusetts Board of Education in 1848:

> I believed then (1837), as now, that sectarian books and sectarian instruction, if their encroachment were not resisted, would prove to overthrow of schools.
>
> I believed then, as now, that religious instruction in our schools, to the extent which the Constitution and the laws of the State allowed and prescribed, was indispensable to their highest welfare, and essential to the vitality of moral education. . . .
>
> Our system earnestly inculcates all Christian morals; it founds its morals on the basis of religion; it welcomes the religion of the Bible, and in receiving the Bible, it allows it to do what is allowed to do in no other system, to speak for itself.[1]

Mann envisioned using the Bible, devoid of sectarian commentary, as a means to teach moral values in common schools. His only stated legal concern was to stay within the bounds imposed by *state* constitutional and statutory law.

The allegedly nonsectarian use of the Bible and Christian moral instruction in Massachusetts common schools led to controversy. During much of the nineteenth century, minority Roman Catholics objected to the public school use of both Protestant versions of the Bible and Protestant-leaning textbooks. When Catholics took over the school committee in heavily immigrant Boston in the 1880s, it was the Protestants' turn to complain. A nationally publicized controversy arose when the new school committee removed an allegedly anti-Catholic history textbook from the public schools. The Protestant-backed Boston Evangelical Alliance responded with a public campaign that simultaneously denounced the school committee's actions as sectarian and called for public school instruction in nonsectarian Christian principles. Petitions circulated by the alliance also endorsed a federal constitutional amendment preventing local public schools from promoting sectarian religious beliefs.

Such an amendment was first proposed on the national level by President Ulysses S. Grant a decade earlier. In a message to Congress in 1875 Grant stated: "I suggest for your earnest consideration—and most earnestly recommend—a constitutional amendment making it the duty of each of the several States to establish and forever maintain free public schools . . . [and] forbidding the teaching in said schools of religious, atheistic, or pagan tenets."[2] Subsequent efforts to adopt such an amendment were led by the Republican leader of the U.S. House of Representatives, James G. Blaine. Indeed, so vigorous were Blaine's efforts that the proposal became known as the "Blaine amendment." Although Blaine was primarily concerned with barring public financing for Roman Catholic schools, which were then being opened in increasing numbers throughout the country, his amendment reached further. It would have generally precluded states from enacting "any law respecting an establishment of religion" and also specifically forbade both public support for religious organizations and religious tests for holding state office.[3]

The text of the amendment and Blaine's comments about it strongly suggest that supporters wanted something stricter than the existing federal establishment clause to deal with growing concern about Roman Catholic education. Indeed, the resulting perception that Blaine and his amendment were anti-Catholic contributed to his narrow defeat for the presidency in 1884 and to the repeated failure of the amendment to pass in Congress by the requisite two-thirds margin.

The acrimony that dogged and ultimately defeated the Blaine amendment stemmed from its nativist undertones.

A common school movement had been growing at the local and state levels in many parts of the country for at least half a century before the introduction of the Blaine amendment. In part, this movement supported free public education to assimilate the increasingly diverse immigrant groups then entering the United States in steadily multiplying numbers. To achieve this objective, the states and local governments moved away from sectarian instruction and toward the teaching of core community values, which were often explicitly Christian and implicitly Protestant. Many Roman Catholics, especially Irish immigrants protective of their religious and ethnic traditions, found the resulting common schools unacceptable. Some sought a share of public education funds to support their own schools. Common school advocates resisted these efforts, leading many states in the mid-1800s to adopt legal and constitutional restrictions against both the use of public funds for sectarian schools and the sectarian control of public schools. President Grant and Representative Blaine led the national government's foray into this controversy by advocating a federal constitutional amendment limiting state support of sectarian education.

Nativist appeals and accusations marked the congressional debate over the Blaine amendment. For example, while the original amendment was still pending in the House, opponent Rep. S. S. Cox decried "a sinister sentiment of religious bigotry" behind the proposal, and supporter Rep. Henry W. Blair denounced Roman Catholic efforts to undermine the common school movement. In the Senate, Frederick T. Frelinghuysen, a leading member of the committee that drafted the Senate version of the amendment and later president of the American Bible Society, assured members that the proposal would not prevent teaching that "pure and undefiled religion which appertains to the relationship and responsibility of man to God, and is readily distinguishable from the creeds of sects." According to Frelinghuysen, the pure religion, "which is our history" and should be taught in public schools, "is a very, very different thing from the particular creeds or tenets of either religionists or infidels." Without expressly identifying any wrongful sectarian instruction, the ensuing debate repeatedly focused on the divisiveness of separate schools for Roman Catholics.[4]

Even though the letter of the Blaine amendment never became part of the U.S. Constitution, its spirit influenced later state constitutions. This influence took two forms. First, new states were typically required to implement a modified version of the Blaine amendment as a condition of joining the Union. Second, both old and new states voluntarily added such restrictions to their state constitutions. Washington State, for example, was influenced in both ways. The 1889 federal statute enabling the admission of Washington to the Union required that the state provide "for the establishment and maintenance of systems of public schools free from sectarian control."[5] Delegates at the ensuing state constitutional convention went even further toward imposing Blaine amendment restrictions upon their new state. This is apparent from their treatment of both education and religion in the state constitution.

The delegates clearly expressed their views on education: they valued it highly. Indeed, their "Preamble" to the education article of the state constitution declares: "It is the paramount duty of the state to make ample provisions for the education of all children residing within its borders, without distinction or preference on account of race, color, caste, or sex."[6] This clause of the state constitution elevated the education of children above all other state functions. Indeed, one of the leading delegates to the convention,

Tacoma attorney Theodore L. Stiles, later wrote: "No other state has placed the common school on so high a pedestal. One who carefully reads Article IX might also wonder whether, after giving to the school fund all that is here required to be given, anything would be left for other purposes."[7]

Significantly, nothing in this preamble restricts state support for education to the instruction provided by public schools. The text confers a right on *all* children residing in Washington, not solely on public school students. Even though section 2 of the education article suggests that the right can be satisfied by providing "a general and uniform system of public schools," the state is not precluded from doing more. Indeed, the plain language of the state constitution and the apparent intent of the people who wrote and ratified it is that the state should do all that it can to promote the education of all children residing within its borders. It seems, therefore, that if Washington State lawmakers today reasonably believe that a school-choice program would advance this goal of promoting education *generally*, and not just serve the interests of so-called sectarian schools, then such a program should accord with the original intent of these provisions of the state constitution.

Following this preamble expressing general support for education, the text of the education article deals with public schools and their funding. The state legislature is directed to provide for a system of public schools, including common schools, high schools, normal schools, and technical schools, and state funds are set aside to support these public schools. These funds are clearly not to be invaded to obtain support for private schools. But nothing in the language of this article or the surviving convention history suggests that other state funds could not be used to support private education.

The state constitution's special establishment clause for education appears in the midst of this article. It is placed between two sections dealing with the creation and preservation of separate state funds for public education. In context, its proscription that "[a]ll schools maintained or supported wholly or in part by the public funds shall be forever free from sectarian control or influence," applies to institutions within the public school system. Some of these schools, such as common schools, were maintained wholly by direct public funds; others, such as normal and technical schools, were maintained in part by direct public funds and in part by student tuition. State colleges were also supported by both direct public funds and student tuition. All these schools were to be forever free from sectarian control or influence.

The history of the special establishment clause supports this reading of the text. The exact language was lifted from a model constitution proposed for Washington by a prominent California attorney and state constitution expert, W. Lair Hill. Hill's commentary accompanying his special establishment clause states: "This section is taken from the constitution of Illinois, modified only so far as it seems necessary to bring it into conformity to the provisions on this subject in the act of Congress providing for the admission of the state."[8] Relevant portions of both the Illinois constitution and the Federal Enabling Act deal exclusively with the creation of public schools and never mention the issue of additional state support for private or parochial schools. In particular, the Illinois constitution simply required that the state provide "a thorough and efficient system of free schools." Similarly, the Federal Enabling Act mandates "the establishment and maintenance of a system of public schools, which shall be open to all children . . . and free from sectarian control." Here, it is especially clear that the ban against sectarianism is aimed at public schools, and not at private schools.

The decision and debate at the state constitutional convention over the special establishment clause reflect this understanding of the clause's aim and reach. The delegates were principally concerned with sectarian or religious activities within the constitutionally mandated system of public schools supported by specially designated state education funds. In an era when prayer and Bible reading were common activities in public schools, this was a significant area of concern in and of itself. They did not intend to address the additional issue of state aid for students attending private schools. This issue was covered by the general establishment clause, which the convention had already included in the state constitution's opening "Preamble and Declaration of Rights." The general establishment clause specifically precludes public money or property being "appropriated for or applied to any religious worship, exercise or instruction, or the support of any religious establishment."[9]

It was only natural at the time for the delegates to include religious instruction as one of the activities targeted for restriction. The 1889 Washington State Constitutional Convention was dominated by Republicans. At the time, the GOP was split into three hostile factions, with Blaine leading one of them. Washington delegations to Republican National Conventions solidly supported Blaine each time that he ran for the presidential nomination from 1876 through 1892. In doing so, they inevitably endorsed Blaine's crusade against government financing for religious instruction. In promoting this position, Blaine did not intend to express hostility to either education or religion. Quite to the contrary, Blaine was a strong supporter of both education and religion; he simply opposed diverting any public support from basic, common school education to what he and others considered to be narrow sectarian instruction. Proponents of the Blaine amendment generally held this view.

It is likely that delegates to the Washington State Constitutional Convention also shared it. They clearly expressed their support for education by declaring that the state's paramount duty was to provide for the education of all children within its borders. They added their continuous approval of religion both through the language of the constitution's preamble (which after much debate expressly followed the precedent of all other state constitutions by acknowledging a divine source for government authority) and through their hard-fought decision to permit property tax exemptions for religious institutions. Yet they clearly favored a stricter establishment clause than was provided by the federal Constitution.

The conclusion that the Washington state constitution's establishment clauses are stricter than the establishment clause in the federal Constitution is confirmed by an interesting series of recent court decisions involving Larry Witters. As a blind person, Witters was eligible for vocational rehabilitation funds from the Washington State Commission for the Blind. He applied for such funds in 1979 to pursue postsecondary training at a Bible college to prepare for a career as a pastor. After the commission rejected this application on *state* constitutional grounds, Witters appealed. In its first disposition of the case, the state supreme court affirmed the commission's decision on *federal* constitutional grounds alone.[10]

The U.S. Supreme Court unanimously reversed this decision, holding that, under the federal Constitution, a vocational rehabilitation program generally serving blind students can finance an eligible recipient's training at a religious institution for a religious career. Indeed, this decision offers precedent for upholding any truly neutral form of school-choice program under the federal Constitution. However, the High Court remanded the case to the state supreme court, stating that "the state court is of course free to consider the applicability of the 'far stricter' dictates of the Washington State Constitution."[11]

Citing the "sweeping and comprehensive" state constitutional proscription against appropriating and applying public funds for religious instruction, and characterizing this as "a major difference between our state constitution and the establishment clause of the First Amendment to the United States Constitution," the state supreme court reaffirmed the agency decision in 1989, this time solely on *state* constitutional grounds.[12] The U.S. Supreme Court denied Witters' petition for further review, thereby leaving the state ban in place. Thus, through this disposition of Larry Witters' case, both federal and state supreme courts confirm the conclusion that the establishment clauses of the Washington state constitution can and do erect a higher wall of separation between church and state than is raised by the federal Constitution.

The final resolution of the Witters litigation provides the framework for analyzing the validity of any school-choice program under the Blaine amendment provisions of the Washington state constitution as currently interpreted. Since the Washington constitution is viewed as one of the strictest on this point, it also suggests the parameters of the state constitutional barriers to parochial school aid generally. In ultimately denying student aid from the state to Witters, the court wrote: "Here, the applicant is asking the State to pay for a religious course of study at a religious school, with a religious career as his goal. This falls precisely within the clear language of the state constitutional prohibition against applying public moneys to any religious instruction."[13] This carefully worded passage stresses that Witters was ineligible for state aid because he was enrolled in "a religious course of study at a religious school, with a religious career as a goal." Nothing in this language suggests that Witters would have been ineligible for the aid had he enrolled in a course of study designed to prepare him for a "secular" career regardless of whether he was enrolled at a religious school. Enrollment at a religious school was simply one factor that contributed to the outcome; it was not alone decisive.

More critically, the case involved a patently "religious school," the Inland Empire School of the Bible, not simply a parochial or church-related institution. The significance of this is highlighted by the fact that Witters had applied for state vocational rehabilitation funds to pursue a joint program at Inland Empire School of the Bible and Whitworth College. The decision voices no concern about Witters' attendance at Whitworth College even though that college is a church-related institution. Indeed, in an earlier case, *Weiss* v. *Bruno,* the Washington state supreme court specifically acknowledged that Whitworth College and every other private accredited college and university in Washington were subject to some degree of sectarian control or influence. In that 1973 decision, this finding was sufficient to preclude state aid exclusively for and directly to those institutions.[14] But *Witters* does not suggest that students attending those schools are automatically ineligible to receive state vocational rehabilitation funds. Quite to the contrary, eligible recipients regularly receive state aid under programs like those for the blind that go to students for secular instruction regardless of whether they attend public or private institutions. In effect, these are special school-choice programs for a limited group of recipients because those recipients are free to choose their school, including one that is church-related.

Here then is the lesson of *Witters* for a school-choice program. Even an intentionally neutral state-funded program, which truly treats public school and private school students equally, may not pay for "religious" instruction. The stricter, more specific provisions of the state constitution's general establishment clause prohibits such payments even though the federal constitution's establishment clause does not. The *Witters* decision conclusively presumes that "a religious course of study at a religious school, with a religious career as a goal" constitutes religious instruction.[15]

A school-choice program for elementary and secondary school students should be subject to the same constitutional standards as one for postsecondary students, such as the program at issue in *Witters.* Both types involve the payment of public money for school instruction. Nothing in the state constitution's general or special establishment clauses limits those provisions to elementary and secondary education. Indeed, the state supreme court in *Weiss* applied the same standard to strike down both a program to provide state aid to students at parochial elementary and secondary schools and a program to provide such aid to students at "sectarian" colleges and universities. *Weiss* found that *both* programs ran afoul of the state constitution's special establishment clause for education.

Thus, we are driven back to *Witters,* which raises barriers to private school students participating in a school-choice program *only* to the extent that they are receiving religious instruction. There is no reason to presume, however, that students are receiving religious instruction when they are taking basic education courses taught by state-certified teachers at state-approved private schools. Yet, by state law, such coursework constitutes the bulk of the instruction provided at private schools. The situation is analogous to the case of postsecondary students eligible for vocational rehabilitation funds or other aid under one of the current state programs for the physically or economically disadvantaged. Those students could choose to use their state funds for nonreligious instruction at a properly accredited church-related college. The institution need only separate the tuition and other charges to insure that no public moneys are paid for religious instruction. The same should be true at the elementary and secondary school levels. Indeed, by requiring that the curriculum of all state-approved private schools should include specific basic education courses taught by state-certified teachers, Washington has clearly delineated what in its view is a nonreligious element of the instruction offered by private schools. Within the parameters suggested by *Witters*, vouchers could be used to pay for this nonreligious instruction provided that it was segregated from any religious elements of the curriculum. Of course, such segregation is not always possible. That apparently was part of the problem in *Witters*, when the majority on the state court found that all Witters' Bible school courses "necessarily provide indoctrination in the specific beliefs of Christianity."[16] But this need no more be true of all the coursework at a state-approved parochial school than it is at a properly accredited church-related college.

A further constraint on state aid for parochial school students is suggested by *Weiss v. Bruno*. As discussed above, *Weiss* voided a pair of parochial school aid programs under the special establishment clause requirement that "[a]ll schools maintained or supported wholly or in part by the public funds shall be forever free from sectarian control or influence." This clause was not used by the state supreme court in *Witters*, and should not apply for any programs, such as the vocational rehabilitation program at issue in *Witters*, where eligible recipients of state funds are truly free to spend them at a variety of public and private schools. In such a case, the state is not maintaining or supporting any schools. Quite to the contrary, the state is intending to support particular needy recipients, who in turn use their state support to purchase educational services.

The situation was very different in *Weiss*, which involved programs designed primarily to assist students at private schools and colleges. Under the college program, *all* of the funds were designated to support students at private colleges and universities in Washington, all of which were judged to be subject to sectarian control or influence. Under the elementary and secondary school program, 85 percent of the funds were allocated to support students at private schools in Washington, nearly all of which were parochial. Thus, the clear intent and primary effect of both programs were to channel money through students to parochial schools and sectarian colleges. That is neither the intent nor the effect of a true public *and* private school-choice program.

A school-choice program is designed to empower parents to choose their child's school and, by doing so, to give all schools a financial incentive to improve. To achieve this result, public money to support the child's education must follow that child regardless of whether the parents choose a public or a private school. The money cannot simply go to private schools, as occurred in *Weiss*, because this would deprive public schools of an equal financial incentive to attract students. For purposes of Washington's special establishment clause, public funds distributed under a true public and private school-choice program would support a student's education—not any particular schools. Similarly, for purposes of the general establishment clause, the application of public money for instruction in a parochial school is the result of personal decisions by the individual recipients, not by the state.

The Washington state constitution, as drafted by its framers and currently interpreted by the state supreme court, imposes substantial, specific restriction on public support for private education, especially at parochial schools. Indeed, it carries through the spirit of the Blaine amendment, which has influenced many American state constitutions. This does not necessarily betray hostility toward either private education or religion, however. It reflects a deep and unwavering commitment to the paramount value of a basic education for all children. A true public and private school-choice program may reflect a similar commitment to education. As long as all state aid follows individual students to their chosen public or private school and is not diverted either from other funds for public education or to finance religious instruction, then the program should conform to the Washington state constitution and the Blaine amendment. It is unlikely that any other state constitution imposes stricter limits.

3

School Vouchers and the United States Constitution

Phillip E. Johnson

ocialism—in the sense of state monopoly—is an unpopular doctrine in the United States, but our opinion-molders are devout state monopolists when it comes to education. We should not be surprised that American public education is a failing enterprise, for it is managed like Soviet agriculture in the period of stagnation. State monopoly is the rule and the ideal; private choice is the grudgingly tolerated exception.

The apparatchiks of education justify their monopoly power just as their Soviet counterparts used to do, by telling us that choice and competition will lead to inequality and exploitation. Some students will learn too much; others will lag behind. Bureaucrats usually prefer equality in mediocrity under their own management to diversity of achievement under conditions of freedom. They also have a very low opinion of the people over whom they rule. Our rulers of education insist that American parents are incorrigible racists who will resegregate society if given the opportunity. On the other hand, these same rulers also oppose choice even when it is offered specifically to inner-city racial minorities who are learning next to nothing in the state schools. The teachers' unions and civil rights lawyers sincerely want disadvantaged minority children to get a good education, but only under the management of the state monopolists. If educational reform means allowing private providers, and especially Christian schools, to show that they can do a better job, they want none of it.

The opponents of choice in education are teachers and intellectuals, members of what Peter Berger and others have called the "knowledge class."[1] The knowledge class is highly skilled at manipulating concepts and definitions, and it regards the religion of the ordinary people as so much harmful superstition. It is not surprising that members of this elite have managed to convince themselves that their own attitudes about education and religion are enshrined in the U.S. Constitution.

The First Amendment says that *Congress* may not pass a law "respecting an establishment of religion, or prohibiting the free exercise thereof." The amendment's language unmistakably conveys its original purpose, which was to prevent the federal government from making laws about religion, and thus to leave this subject to state and local authorities. After the Second World War, however, a series of Supreme Court decisions, culminating in the "school prayer" and "Bible reading" cases of 1963,[2] turned the establishment clause on its head. Intended as a restriction on the federal government, it became instead an open-ended charter for the federal judiciary to impose on local school boards its own vision of the proper relationship between religion and the people. Of course, that vision has turned out to embody the agnostic viewpoint of the knowledge class. The public schools, which are the only schools available to most non-wealthy people today, are resolutely secular. Parents who choose a religious education for their children must pay the full cost, while they are also paying taxes to educate the children of their neighbors. Secularist organizations like the American Civil Liberties Union insist that the Constitution requires this inequitable situation, although, as we shall see, some Supreme Court decisions take a much more flexible approach.

The religion clauses of the federal Constitution are stated in broad language, which does not refer specifically to topics like "education" or "public funds." Some state constitutions contain more specific language relating to religion and public education. For example, as Edward Larson explained, the Washington state constitution provides in Article I, Section 11 that "No public money shall be appropriated for or applied to any religious worship, exercise, or instruction, or the support of any religious establishment." Another section says that "All schools maintained wholly or in part by the public funds shall be forever free from sectarian control or influence." These provisions date from the time of Washington's admission to the Union in 1889, and they clearly contemplate the existence of state schools maintained by tax funds, which should provide no religious instruction and remain free of all sectarian influence.[3]

The state provisions have taken on particular importance today because the United States Supreme Court seems no longer to be as firmly committed to the "wall of separation" ideology in church-state matters as it once was. In particular, there are signs that several justices, perhaps a majority, would hold that the First Amendment's establishment clause permits a state to provide tuition vouchers to parents or students to use at the schools of their choice, including religious schools. This development is welcomed both by those who want parents to be able to choose a religious education, and by those who just want to open up the education industry to competition in the hope of increasing its efficiency. But voucher programs cannot get off the ground until and unless the role of religious schools is settled. The question, then, is whether the state provisions constitute an insuperable obstacle to programs of free choice in education through tuition vouchers, even assuming that the federal constitutional objections have been overcome.

My answer is that the state provisions are not as powerful an obstacle as they may appear to be. Essentially the same interpretive questions arise under both the general language of the federal Constitution and the more specific language of some of the state constitutions. If state court decisions interpreting state constitutions are different from the decisions of the United States Supreme Court interpreting the First Amendment, this is primarily because of differences in judicial attitudes rather than differences in constitutional language. Nothing in Washington's constitution, for example, forbids school voucher programs unless a majority of the Washington Supreme Court wants it to do so. Consider again now the saga of Larry Witters, whose court case Larson described in Chapter 1.

In the first court decision dealing with Witters' appeal for public funds to attend a Christian college,[4] the Washington Supreme Court put aside the state constitutional issues and decided on federal constitutional grounds that Witters could receive no state assistance. It found the governing federal standard in a 1971 decision called *Lemon* v. *Kurtzman*, where the Supreme Court had set out a famous three-part test for determining whether a state statute was consistent with the First Amendment's establishment clause: "First, the statute must have a secular legislative purpose; second, its principal or primary effect must be one that neither advances nor inhibits religion . . . ; finally, the statute must not foster 'an excessive government entanglement with religion.'"[5]

The majority opinion of the Washington court acknowledged that the vocational rehabilitation program had a secular purpose, and it did not reach the murky question of "entanglement." It did hold, however, that providing assistance to a blind person studying to become a minister would violate the second "prong" of the *Lemon* test. In the Washington court's words, "the providing of financial assistance by the State to enable someone to become a pastor, missionary, or church youth director clearly has the primary effect of advancing religion."

In a sense, it does. But that way of putting the question makes it sound as if the legislature had enacted a private bill to allow Larry Witters to become a minister. On the contrary, the legislation in question was a general program of vocational assistance for the visually handicapped, to allow such persons to become financially self-supporting by preparing for careers of their own choice. If we limit our vision to the single case of Larry Witters, the subsidy seems like a benefit to religion. If we look at the program as a whole, it is obvious that religious careers and religious education were neither encouraged nor discouraged. What would destroy this fair balance, and involve the state in discrimination against religious choices, would be a policy of denying equal treatment to persons who choose religious careers.

Remember, the *Lemon* test supposedly bars both advancement *and* inhibition of religion evenhandedly. Some blind persons may go to seminary to become pastors; others may go to journalism school to learn to write publishable articles attacking religion as the opium of the people. What ought to raise a constitutional question is a state policy of subsidizing one of those alternatives but not the other.

That brings us to a theoretical point about interpretation. Concepts like aiding or hindering religion have meaning only in relationship to some assumed reference point that defines "neutrality." For example, the section of the Washington constitution that prohibits the use of public money for religion also contains a specific exception allowing the state to employ chaplains for prisons and mental institutions. Providing chaplains obviously advantages religion in comparison to not employing chaplains, but that is not the appropriate comparison. By putting people in prison, or inducting them into the military, the government disrupts whatever access to religious programs they might otherwise have. In context, providing chaplains of many denominations is a rough attempt to restore the *status quo ante,* not favoritism to religion. That is why provision of chaplains in the military and prisons (unlike provision of chaplains to say opening prayers at legislative sessions) is not a matter of any great constitutional controversy.[6]

Government also provides services like roads and public libraries. People ride city buses on city streets to go to church or parochial school, and the public library stocks the works of C. S. Lewis as well as those of Bertrand Russell. If someone were to propose barring all "religious" books from the public libraries, we would all see the proposal as censorship and a discriminatory attack upon religion. The reason is that in libraries, our assumed standard of reference is equal treatment of religion and nonreligion, not "secular only."

As the original decision in the *Witters* case illustrates, however, many people assume a different reference point when it comes to the provision of education. For those people, "neutrality" in education does mean "secular only," rather than evenhanded treatment of religious and secular education. Why the difference? Before answering that question I want to describe the second *Witters* decision, in which the United States Supreme Court unanimously reversed the state court decision previously described.[7]

All nine Supreme Court justices agreed in *Witters II* that the state court decision in *Witters I* was wrong, but the Supreme Court split almost down the middle on the rationale. No justice thought that the State of Washington would be establishing a religion if it permitted a single blind person to obtain a religious education at public expense. What divided the Court—and led organizations like the American Civil Liberties Union to urge affirmation of the state decision—was that the militant secularists saw the specter of school vouchers lurking in the background. If Larry Witters could use state funds to pay tuition at a Bible college, could a state enact a general tuition subsidy program that would allow parents to choose a religious education for their children?

Justice Marshall's majority opinion tried to rule for Larry Witters on the narrowest possible grounds. The opinion explained that it is not only direct payments to churches or religious schools that violate the First Amendment. Tuition subsidies or tax benefits that went to parents or students, who then used them at the school of their choice, had been held unconstitutional in some previous cases on the theory that they amounted to a disguised subsidy of religion.[8] On the other hand, Justice Marshall acknowledged that "the Establishment Clause is not violated every time money previously in the possession of a state is conveyed to a religious institution." For example, persons receiving salaries or pensions from the state may donate the money to a church, and the state may continue to pay them even if it knows what they plan to do with the money.

When does a private decision to use a state educational subsidy at a religious school become a disguised subsidy? Justice Marshall's opinion suggested that the constitutionality of a program to subsidize individuals depends upon how *many* of those individuals are going to make payments to some religious institution. Previous Supreme Court decisions had held private school tuition subsidy programs unconstitutional where the overwhelming majority of the private schools in the state were religious schools, specifically Roman Catholic schools. The effect of a voucher-style subsidy in such cases was substantially the same in financial impact as a direct payment from the state to the Catholic school system. In contrast, most blind persons in Washington would undoubtedly use vocational rehabilitation assistance for secular purposes, and therefore only a trivial percentage of the expended funds would find their way to religious coffers. According to Justice Marshall's line of reasoning, a state could include religious alternatives in a general publicly financed program only if not many persons were likely to choose them.

Five justices (a majority of the Court) joined concurring opinions objecting to the narrowness of the holding. Each of the concurring opinions specifically objected to the majority's failure to cite a 1983 decision called *Mueller* v. *Allen*. In that case the Supreme Court had upheld (by a 5–4 vote) a Minnesota statute providing tax deductions for certain educational expenses, including tuition at private schools. About 90 percent of the private schools in question were religious schools, and Justice Marshall's dissent had vehemently argued that the decision to uphold the Minnesota plan was not easy to reconcile with the logic of some earlier and more restrictive tuition subsidy cases. One of the concurring opinions in *Witters* explained that the *Mueller* holding had, by implication, rejected Marshall's suggestion that the Washington program was constitutional only because very few handicapped persons were likely to choose a religious education. "Over 90% of the tax benefits in *Mueller* ultimately flowed to religious institutions. . . . Nevertheless, the aid was thus channeled by individual parents and not by the State, making the tax deduction permissible under the 'primary effect' test of *Lemon.*"[9]

Mueller v. Allen involved a subsidy to education by tax deductions, and not a direct subsidy by voucher. Even with that qualification in mind, it is reasonable to infer that as of 1986, five Supreme Court justices were inclined to uphold programs allowing parents or students to choose between secular and religious schools, even where the practical outcome was that many parents would choose in favor of religion. Since that time Justices Burger, Powell, Brennan, and Marshall have left the Court, and their replacements are Justices Scalia, Kennedy, Souter, and Thomas. The winds of change are blowing fiercely at the Supreme Court,[10] and advocates of voucher programs have every reason to be encouraged.

But what about that Washington state constitutional provision, which forbids spending state money on religious education in much more specific language than the establishment clause of the federal Constitution? Addressing that question brings me to *Witters III*, the third decision in the case.

The Supreme Court's majority opinion in *Witters II* refused to decide whether the state would violate Witters' constitutional rights under the free exercise or equal protection clauses if it excluded him from educational benefits pursuant to state law. Instead, the majority remanded the case to the Washington Supreme Court for a determination on any remaining issues. By a narrow majority, the Washington court held that paying for Witters to go to Bible college would violate the state constitution's explicit ban on state appropriations for "religious instruction."[11]

That is the bad news; the good news is that four of the nine Washington justices dissented. Shift one vote and the Washington constitution would mean something very different. Two dissenting opinions said that no appropriation for religious instruction is involved when aid for education is made available to individual students to use for vocational education of their choosing. Two opinions also said that the state violated Witters' rights under the federal free exercise clause by singling out his educational program for unfavorable treatment.

The Supreme Court refused to hear the case again after the state court's decision in *Witters III,* but there are sound reasons for predicting that a majority of the justices would uphold Witters' free exercise claim if the Court were to decide a similar case on the merits today. Unlike some other litigants who have unsuccessfully invoked the free exercise clause, Larry Witters was not seeking some special exemption from a law of general applicability.[12] He was seeking equal treatment in comparison to blind persons with secular ambitions, and it is difficult to see what "compelling interest" the state would have in denying him benefits. That the payment would violate some provision of the state constitution is not in itself a compelling state interest.[13]

The lesson I draw from the Witters saga and the rest of First Amendment religious law is that no constitutional language—state or federal—explicitly tells us whether a state may provide vouchers to students or parents to use for tuition at the school of their choice. If you think that secu-

lar education should be encouraged and religious education discouraged, probably because you are not an admirer
of the kind of religion you suspect most parents will choose,
your constitutional argument is clear. The money flows from
the recipients to the schools they choose, which are often
or mostly religious schools, and so the economic effect is
not very different from that of a direct subsidy to the same
schools. You can further justify your conclusion by arguing
that taxpayers should not have to support a religion with
which they disagree, even though taxpayers who disagree
with what is being taught in the public schools have to pay
regardless.

If, on the other hand, you think that parents and students
should be able to choose freely between religious and secular schools, your argument is equally clear. When the state
gives tax benefits or vouchers to students or parents for educational purposes, the money involved becomes *their* money,
not the state's. Their choice to spend the money for one kind
of school rather than another involves no state appropriation or funding decision. If church schools end up with the
money it is because they are providing an educational service that the consumers desire to purchase, and secular
providers are free to compete with them on exactly the same
terms. From the prochoice point of view, the overall meaning of the religion clauses in education is not "secular only"
but rather freedom to choose between religious and secular education.

The prochoice argument is not weakened if it happens
that *most* parents or students choose to use their vouchers
at religious schools. Any preponderance in favor of that
alternative simply measures the sum of private choices by
free individuals; it does not reflect any state policy of favor-
ing religion. The argument is not even affected if the state
has chosen to offer the voucher alternative specifically

because it knows that many parents prefer religious schools, and wants to make them free to exercise that preference. The *Lemon* test tells us that the state may not use its legislative power for the purpose of aiding religion, but the state may certainly enact legislation to further the *free exercise* of religion, which is a purpose of the First Amendment itself. From the prochoice viewpoint, what is constitutionally suspect is not the furthering of educational choice, but the refusal to allow choice, especially when that refusal is motivated by hostility to religion.

What can those of us who favor choice do to persuade the courts to uphold voucher systems? The first thing is that we should refuse to be fooled by the claim that "secular only" is either required by the Constitution or genuinely "neutral" on questions of religion. The schools of today try to teach children everything they really need to know—not just the three R's, but subjects such as automobile driving, values clarification, and how to have sex without getting AIDS. The clear premise of the system is that what is excluded from the curriculum—God, for example—is either pernicious or unnecessary. The schools do not teach that God created us, but they emphatically teach what did, namely, naturalistic evolution, which got along just fine without God's help. The same schools that would not dream of having Bible readings present as "science" the lavish *Cosmos* series that begins with astronomer Carl Sagan's ringing metaphysical claim that "The Cosmos is all that is, or ever was, or ever will be." Whether this kind of education is good or bad may be debatable, but it certainly is not neutral.

The dominance of "secular only" in public education reflects not our tradition of religious tolerance, but a history of religious conflict in which a coalition of Protestants, Jews, and agnostics inflicted a humiliating defeat upon the Roman Catholics. Until fairly recently, the public schools in most communities were controlled not by bureaucrats, professional politicians, and teachers' unions, but by school boards composed of local citizens. These schools were not so much secular as loosely Protestant, and most people thought they were reasonably effective in teaching the basic academic subjects and in promoting democratic values. Catholics were the only large religious group that thought it necessary to maintain their own schools. Non-Catholics satisfied with public education accordingly thought of religious schools in general as "sectarian," and saw no reason to aid the efforts of the Catholic Church to maintain its authority. The court cases that appealed to the "wall of separation" doctrine thus represented the capture of the judiciary by opponents of Catholic education, and eventually by elements in the knowledge class that hope to relegate all theistic religion to a marginal and thus harmless position in society.

Since the 1960s the triumph of a more militant secularism in the public schools has been consolidated. The superficial signs of this consolidation include the banning of school prayers, Bible readings, and Christian programs. The much more profound change is in the adoption of a moral and intellectual relativism that affects every aspect of school life. Today, many parents choose a religious education for their children even though they themselves regard the religion itself with indifference. They recognize that a school has to believe in *something* in order to have the self-confidence necessary to tell rebellious youngsters that they must apply themselves to learn important things whether they want to or not. Public schools are increasingly perceived as anarchic, drug-ridden, politicized, and permissive. Many parents want their children to get the kind of education public schools provided a couple of generations ago. If it is possible to found a sect upon principles of relativism and permissiveness, then the state schools of today have become sectarian schools.

The history of legal resistance to assisting Roman Catholic schools suggests an important point of strategy. The practice of constitutional law is a special form of politics, and in politics it is always important to have as many allies as possible. I am not using the word "politics" in any pejorative or cynical sense. To say that constitutional lawmaking is a form of politics is simply to say that life is too complicated to be adequately captured in legal concepts like "religious establishment" and "freedom of choice." Behind these formulas there are complex networks of meaning, and the judges who are charged with interpreting that meaning quite naturally trust some people and some groups more than others.

Let me make that general point thoroughly concrete. Roman Catholics in the days before Vatican II could not successfully appeal to "freedom of choice" because so many Protestants and religious Jews—unwisely, in my opinion—feared the Catholic Church much more than they feared the agnostics who were working so successfully to ensure a victory for "secular only." The Supreme Court decisions that held choice plans unconstitutional reflected the same political context. The people who control the spending of tax money are understandably reluctant to turn over some of their power to other people whom they regard as unreasonable and authoritarian. To make "freedom of choice" generally attractive, it has to be apparent that more than one kind of person wants to choose.

Today it is Protestant fundamentalists and evangelicals who are often marginalized, because the knowledge class sees them as a narrow and prejudiced interest group. Agnostic intellectuals are easily persuaded that people who opt for Christian schools must be fleeing from racial integration, or are not really exercising free choice because they are dominated by an authoritarian preacher. Freedom of choice will become irresistible only when it becomes impossible to deny that a great many people of diverse ethnic and religious backgrounds want to have an alternative to the public schools. To put it simply, the independent school movement needs multiethnic and multireligious support, and it needs to be making a very visible contribution to the socially vital work of educating underprivileged youngsters. I believe that many independent schools are doing just that to a much greater extent than most people realize; the challenge is to get the public to see these schools as institutions that help solve social problems, not as elitist refuges for people who want to escape those problems.

Properly understood, the constitutional separation of church and state supports the right of students and parents to choose a religious or a secular education on equivalent financial terms. That right will become a reality when the nation's highest judges learn that "secular only" is not religious neutrality, nor is it in furtherance of religious freedom. It is a formula that militant secularists exploit to expand their power to control other people's lives.

4

Educational Freedom with Justice

James W. Skillen

O ur worries about education in the United States today project worries about our children's future—their economic future, their moral future, their civic future. Most parents want their children to receive a good education. From government they expect fair treatment and equal opportunity. They want justice. But justice is a large order, because it requires that each person and institution receive its proper due. In a large and complex society the desire for justice is a difficult desire to satisfy. What would it mean for people to receive their proper due—namely, justice—in the realm of education? What kind of justice does our Constitution permit or require for education?

Historical Orientation

When the United States was founded, schooling was not fixed or structured by a constitutional mandate. Nor was it defined strictly as a government or nongovernment, familial or nonfamilial, religious or nonreligious enterprise. Common law and tradition, reflecting long-term habits of schooling by families, churches, and other agencies, ruled the day. Governments at various times, from the beginning of the colonial era in what is now Massachusetts up to the mid-1800s, passed laws to aid, encourage, or require some schooling of their citizens. But not until the ideas of Thomas Jefferson, Noah Webster, Benjamin Rush, Horace Mann, and others began to take hold in the 1840s (when Boston, New York, and other cities were experiencing rapid social change), did the establishment of a formal system of government-backed common schools begin to define the landscape of American education.[1]

In the mid-nineteenth century, slavery had not yet been rejected nor had religion been redefined as a "sectarian" practice that should be confined to private space. Few, if any, state laws required racial fairness in schooling,[2] and Horace Mann's publicly supported common schools were very religious in a moralistic, Protestant way.[3] Nevertheless, in the 1840s state and local governments began to take initiatives to advance literacy and common schooling that would, over the next century and a half, lead to an ever widening system of uniform, democratically homogeneous, bureaucratically governed schools. In those schools, differences of a religious, racial, familial, or cultural character would be ignored, rejected, or celebrated depending on public governance decisions at the time.[4]

The decisions made by cities and states to establish a government-run system of schools clashed with the religious, economic, and cultural diversity of American society right from the start. Most obvious in the 1840s was the clash of the Protestant majority with a newly immigrating Catholic minority that was streaming into the cities of New York, Boston, and Philadelphia. Those immigrants experienced the new educational establishments as a direct and unjust onslaught on their preferred means of educating their children for public and private life.[5] Was the minority right or wrong? Were they treated justly or unjustly? Was their civic freedom protected or abridged?

In the 1840s the dominant white, Anglo-Saxon, Protestant (WASP) ideal of a coherent society guided majorities in several northern cities and states to take the political step of turning over ultimate responsibility for schooling to their governments. They did this in a manner that purposely excluded Catholic schools, just as slaves were purposely excluded from public schooling in the South. The majority held in its mind not simply the principle of majority rule in politics, but also the conviction that some degree of cultural homogeneity is essential to the maintenance of an ordered society. By force of public law, Catholic schools were defined as private, "sectarian" enterprises undeserving of public, "nonsectarian" support. Catholic schools supposedly threatened the cultural homogeneity of the WASP culture. Catholic schools were not outlawed completely but were denied access to public funding and recognition. The consequence was that public funding was monopolized by governments for the one system of schools run directly by those governments. That system, under state and local law, had as its purpose to train all children into a common way of life.[6]

The government-operated schools were "public" in the sense of being governed directly by public law, even though the "governing" bodies in those days may have been no larger than the city council, the local school board, or the town meeting. The schools that public authorities defined as private and "sectarian" were free for the most part to govern themselves, but they were permitted to exist only on the periphery of public life so as not to interfere with the culturally homogeneous common life directed by the will of its majority. Catholics, in other words, could be citizens as long as their schools, like their churches, confined their activities to a private sphere. Thus, the civic lives of those not party to the majority culture were sharply separated from their private, nonconforming lives.

The Protestant majority did not at first experience such a separation because the Protestantism of the majority (including its King James Bible, moral codes, etc.) remained the governing ethos of the public, "nonsectarian" schools. Not until the 1950s and 1960s would a growing number of Protestants begin to experience the exclusion felt by Catholics in the 1840s. But by the 1960s the system of school governance established by Protestants during the preceding century was firmly established. By the 1960s all traditional religious views were being defined (by majority will and constitutional interpretation) as sectarian and were dismissed from the government's nonsectarian (now "secularized") school system.[7]

By the time governments got serious about redressing the inequities caused by racial discrimination in schooling in the 1950s, the system of government-run schools had been firmly entrenched.[8] Moreover, the so-called nonsectarian public schools were, by this time, so fully conceived as expressions of a popular, majority will that the idea of "justice" was restricted in application to requiring the exclusion from those schools of anything that did not satisfy the civic majority acting through its public legislators and educational officers. For example, only today has the majority begun to notice the inequities involved in deriving school funds by means of property taxes—something that leads to unfair expenditures for rich and poor. It was not until the 1950s that racial discrimination in schools began to be seriously challenged at the federal level. The challenge to racial discrimination, of course, arose very late in the day as far as most African-Americans are concerned. The injustice of channeling public funds only to government schools, however, has still not been redressed because majority opinion and Court rulings have thus far largely supported the nineteenth-century establishment.

The main point to stress here is that the governance of education, from the 1840s on, manifested a highly restrictive vision of justice rooted in the idea that government should act uniformly in accord with majority will to advance a culturally homogeneous *public* program for society. Anything that could not be approved through public governance, and which appeared to exhibit diversifying cultural or religious tendencies, had to be pushed into private space. The typical pattern of action by a government bureaucracy is precisely that it seeks to treat all citizens the same. In the case of education it had, increasingly, to ignore, discredit, or exclude all the dimensions of education over which it was not granted control by legislative, executive, and judicial processes. The full reality of education—as it arose in the culturally diverse circles of America's citizens—inevitably suffered maltreatment at the hands of educational bureaucracies because anything that did not fit the majoritarian, homogenizing mold was discounted or privatized and therefore either squeezed out of government-run schooling or redefined within those schools in ways that would accord with the governing will.

The primary political and governance patterns that have now been established through this historical process are almost never recognized by educational policymakers, reformers, and commentators. Most Americans simply take them for granted. Until we can see those patterns and understand them clearly, however, we will not be able to deal adequately with contemporary injustices in education. The patterns to which I refer are political and legal, more than educational, and arise from a very particular understanding of what should constitute a democratic polity. They actually conflict at many points with the longer-standing and often more complex patterns accepted in the course of the development of American common law.

The newer patterns, already touched on briefly in the discussion above, are those with which Jefferson and Mann operated and which gave birth to the idea of the common school.[9] They are rooted in the idea of the republic as a community whose members govern themselves through their representatives by majority will while recognizing that individuals and minorities should not be tyrannized by the majority in the legitimate enclaves of their private lives. The idea of the democratic republic, in other words, is that of a public order in which justice is achieved when a majority, through due process, rules on any matter it chooses while making room for the private rights of individuals—including the right to opt out of public programs such as government-run schools. Institutions such as families, non-government schools, various voluntary associations, and churches are often, or usually, not recognized as having *both* a function in the public realm *and* an independent, non-government identity. Public laws, it is assumed, may seek to advance a general purpose or benefit without regard to the diversity of nongovernmental institutions even when those institutions are intimately involved in that very public purpose. Anything that the majority chooses not to bring under public rule may be held in private freedom. But the public order is supposed to be a homogeneous, single-willed community. There is no room here for the idea of a pluriform, complex society over which government rules in order to protect and enhance the freedom of its citizens to act *in public* in a diversity of institutional and cultural ways.

From the 1840s onward American schooling got taken up into these patterns of public governance through majoritarian legislation in a manner that radically changed the older and more diverse patterns of schooling that existed before the 1840s.[10] Majority rule for an imagined homogeneous citizenry could, when the popular aim was to promote education for all citizens, ignore or overrule the diverse desires for schooling expressed by nonconforming families, churches, and nongovernment schools. When "the people" decided by government process to offer a civic service, education, their actions were considered good and legitimate by the very definition of a republic. Whatever did not conform to that new, uniformly defined purpose could, with equal legitimacy, be eliminated or relegated to the private sphere. Homogeneity under government; diversity outside government's terrain— that was the heart of the idea. Few if any in the 1840s could (and few today can) conceive that the general public purpose to advance education might better be carried out by public mandates and equitable funding that recognize and promote a diversity of school systems.[11]

Part of the difficulty with the now established patterns is that much of the "ruling" by legislators and governments disrupts and even cripples traditional patterns of responsibility exercised by families, churches, voluntary organizations, and schools in ways that cannot easily be reconsti-

tuted or replicated by government. Insofar as nongovernment institutions have exhibited diversity or dissented from
the majority's decisions about schooling, for example, they
have suffered real discrimination in public. Not only have
their religious, philosophical, or cultural convictions been
thwarted, but they have been put in the position of feeling
alienated (to some degree) from the very democratic polity
to which they belong. The majoritarian process operating
in a political system that aims for the homogeneity of a simple community leads to all-or-nothing decisions. The majority wins control of the public terrain, the minority loses and
retreats into privacy. What government controls by way of
a legislatively initiated, government-conducted program it
controls in a direct programmatic, bureaucratic manner that
may conflict seriously (as it does in the realm of education)
with programs of the same sort that are conducted by nongovernment institutions.

A pluriform or pluralist conception (in contrast to a
majoritarian conception) of a democratic polity requires the
adoption of quite a different posture with respect to the governing of a complex society.[12] It is both more sensitive to
the common law tradition and more alert to the fact that
justice requires fair *public* treatment of the diverse, nonpo-
litical institutions in society and not simply the privatizing
of anything that fails to conform to the programs inaugu-
rated by majority will. In fact, this different conception of
a democratic polity can be illustrated by reference to one of
America's most treasured constitutional settlements—the
disestablishment of the church.

The "Establishment" of Religious Pluralism

The First Amendment to the U.S. Constitution brought
about a certain kind of resolution to a long-standing Euro-

pean and colonial struggle.[13] It said, in effect, that the federal government was not going to treat religious life as a department of state such that a single "program" (church) would be approved by the majority and operated or sustained by government. This also meant, of course, that "the people" would not be allowed to use governmental powers as the means of disapproving, excluding, or discriminating against the nonestablished religious programs. Rather, the federal government would be required by constitutional law to respect the diversity of religious programs entered into by its citizens and would be careful not to give special privilege to any one of them. The actual effect of deciding *not* to allow the establishment of a church or preferred religion by the federal government was to *establish* religious pluralism.[14] This had nothing to do with "secularizing" civic life, as if everything religious could be confined to churches and then privatized. Not until this century did that kind of thinking gain dominance in American public life and public law. What the First Amendment required was that the religious life of American citizens, as they conducted themselves in freely chosen ways—both in public and in private life—would henceforth not be taken up by federal, legislative processes for the purpose of giving privilege to any one of them.

At the same time, however, it was taken for granted that governments *should* act in ways that protected and secured justice for the religious life of citizens carried on in their churches, their families, their schools, and so forth. Henceforth *religious* life (not narrowly defined in terms of church life alone) should be treated in the same way that families were treated in common law, namely, as nongovernmental practices free to occupy public as well as private space, and to be protected and aided by public governance in ways that would enhance their well-being and independence. Families were neither taken over as departments of state nor excluded from all the benefits of public life.[15]

Our First Amendment settlement is what can be called a pluriform or pluralist settlement. Justice entails not only making room for each citizen as a voting individual in the republic, but also securing fair and equitable treatment of all citizens in the free exercise of some of their noncivic duties. No homogenization or uniformity of public program is required. The people's will in governance is fulfilled by means of the constitutional agreement to establish a pluriform or pluralistic system of religious respect. It need go no further. The First Amendment requires neither the privatization of religion nor the homogenization of its practice; rather it gives to religious practice a pluriform public recognition like that enjoyed by families, businesses, and other nongovernmental institutions and communities, assuring religion's free exercise within these and other institutions, independent of direct political control. What is uniform or agreed to through constitutional consensus is that religious pluralism, not religious uniformity, will be established in law.[16]

To the extent that religious practice is given public aid and recognition by government today (through tax relief, utilities services, fire protection, and military chaplaincies for churches), justice can be done only by giving proportionately equitable and fair treatment to all religions (no discrimination) as well as by exercising careful respect for the independent (nongovernmental) character of religious initiatives. It would violate the First Amendment for a civic majority to attempt to use government authority to introduce a religious program that would be granted special favors not accorded to other religious programs. For the government to grant a funding monopoly of any kind to one religion while insisting that others have to operate in private would be to perpetrate injustice. Overcoming precisely that kind of injustice is what the First Amendment does.

With that First Amendment settlement open before us as an illustration of a pluriform or pluralist framework, we are now in a position to expose the injustice of both current American education law (including the so-called Blaine amendment) as well as to chart a course for a redress of those injustices. Before attempting those tasks, however, we must first approach the current circumstances with greater systematic clarity.

The Structural Complexity of Educational Governance

The primary difference between the treatment of churches and the treatment of schools in recent American history is, of course, that America's majority agreed *not* to try to implement public religious programs of a church-type, whereas the majority *did* decide to establish education programs by means of direct government mandate and funding. It is not difficult to understand the motivation for this, and a brief examination of those reasons will help us see the importance of government initiatives in education. That examination will also help expose the structural complexity involved in trying to govern schooling justly.

The U.S. Constitution established a pluriform or pluralist system for religious practice with justice for all. Schooling was not addressed by the federal Constitution except insofar as it recognized that the states and people retained rights and responsibilities not granted to the federal government. In the early years of the new republic, this generally lent support to the ongoing development of a diverse array of practices accepted under common law in the several states, although beginning in the 1840s city and state governments increasingly took legislative action to estab-

lish and govern common schools. Why did governments
become so involved in education?

The answer to that question is not simple, though many
of its dimensions are fairly obvious and well known. Protestant fears of immigrating Catholics suggest one major reason for direct and systematic involvement of government
in the schooling of citizens.[17] But aside from such fears, it
is not hard to see that a society founded upon democratic
governance should be concerned about the literacy and
intelligence of its citizens. Enlightened self-rule surely must
be superior to self-rule in ignorance. Moreover, if a democratic society is highly diverse and is being shaped by a growing number of immigrants from many different cultural and
linguistic backgrounds, one can see the wisdom of civic education that introduces all citizens to a knowledge of the
republic that they share in common. If it is legitimate for
governments to help in the building of roads, sewage systems, and postal communication in order to enhance the
general welfare of the citizenry, then surely it is legitimate
for them to bolster basic literacy and civic education for all
citizens in order to enhance the general welfare and stabil-
ity of the republic.

However, as soon as "the people" begin to legislate schooling, the complexity of society must be sorted out if justice
is to be done. There is nothing in the concern about literacy and civic education, for example, that requires government itself to establish or control the agencies of schooling
or to do all the educating of citizens, any more than it is
necessary for government to build and deliver all the auto-
mobiles in order to license and regulate their use on public
highways for the common good. The fact is that schooling
had been taking place for years before government common
schools were established. None of America's founding
geniuses was educated in the kind of government-run com-

mon school that Jefferson, Mann, and others later sought to establish. Moreover, basic literacy training and general civic education are only part of what most schools and families seek to provide.

Government's initiative on any front, including education, should take into account the responsibility of government to do justice to the manifold responsibilities that people have in society. Questions that ought to be asked include: How should education be justly funded? For how many years of schooling should government subsidies (if any) be provided, and from where should those funds be derived? What is a just system for collecting and distributing education funds? Is it ever just for a government service or requirement to exclude anyone? Should schooling be required of every citizen by force of law or simply offered to those who want it? Should newer immigrants be given extra educational service if they start far below the literacy level of natural-born citizens, or should a standard amount of schooling be offered to every person, regardless of the level at which he or she begins? What about the other institutions and agencies involved in education, such as families, nongovernment schools, churches, and voluntary associations? How can justice be done to all of them?

In the light of these questions, our contention is that justice has not yet been done to the citizens of the United States in regard to education. Without doubt much good has been done through the existing system that gives public privilege to government-run schools and discriminates against nongovernment schools. More citizens may have been helped than hurt by the educational services provided in this manner. But justice still has not been done to all American citizens, and the accumulation of injustice is beginning to undermine public confidence in government's ability to advance the education of all Americans in a sound fashion.

Why has justice not been done to citizens through American education, and what must be done to achieve justice? To lay the groundwork for some programmatic recommendations, let us first mention the actors and dimensions of schooling to which justice must be done.

Constitutionally, justice ought to be done to the religious and expressive freedoms of American citizens as articulated in the First Amendment and now nationalized through the Fourteenth Amendment. Constitutional justice must also be done to the rights and responsibilities of those institutions of the people (families, schools, churches, and voluntarily established organizations) that have not been (or ought not to have been) subsumed under federal or state governments (see the Ninth and Tenth Amendments). Under common law, families, for example, have been, and continue to be, recognized as having responsibility for the well-being of their minor children. These constitutional limits and mandates hold special importance for the public structure of schooling. Finally, justice must also be done to citizens regardless of their racial background, ethnic identity, or gender (Fourteenth, Fifteenth, and Nineteenth Amendments).[18]

In this constitutional context, justice should be exhibited in the manner (due process) in which education is mandated and funded. Taxation and funding should be just both in the way monies are derived and in the way they are distributed. Obviously, majorities will vote on these matters in state legislatures and the federal Congress, but simply getting a majority to vote on something does not make it a just and sound policy. What legislatures and the Congress should be confronted with is more than competing interest-group pleadings; they should hear strong arguments for justice as the reason for voting for one policy over against another.

Toward a System That Assures Justice with Freedom in Education

My argument is that in order for justice to be done to education in a complex society, a fundamental, pluriform transformation of the structure of American schooling is required.[19] This is, I am convinced, something entirely compatible with the Constitution's First Amendment as it now stands, though not necessarily with the way it has been interpreted by some members of the Supreme Court since the 1940s. The changes required to create a pluriform or pluralist system can, therefore, be made by means of legislation at state and local levels coupled, in all probability, with state constitutional changes to alter or eliminate the so-called Blaine amendment. All of this will probably have to be backed up by revised Supreme Court rulings. If the Supreme Court continues to stand opposed to the reasoning that underlies the argument here, then a federal constitutional amendment may be necessary.

What will comprise a pluralist or pluriform system?

Let us begin with the rights of parents that already exist in statutory and common law. My argument is that the legal obligation presently resting on parents or guardians to rear their children should be respected with nondiscriminatory protection. As a right of conscience and parental responsibility all parents should be allowed to select the agencies of their children's education. For that right to be protected fairly, we will have to revise the current discriminatory patterns of the law that thwart parental responsibility.[20]

For example, to the extent that states, for legitimate civic reasons, mandate education for all children, they ought to allow, without any legal or financial discrimination, parental choice of the *means* of schooling, since parents, not the states, hold the principal responsibility for children and

their education. Among other things such nondiscrimination should entail a proportionately fair investment of public educational dollars in every child. The highly inequitable
distribution of educational tax dollars under the current
system of residential, district schools should therefore be
ended. Further, the highly inequitable distribution of school
funds to government-run schools must be stopped. A system of equitable, statewide (or even nationwide) distribution of education dollars to each school-age child (whether
directly or indirectly) regardless of the school he or she
attends should be established. Whether the tax monies are
raised through a property tax or some other means, the distribution should not be allocated on the basis of the residential neighborhood of the child as now occurs. Since religious and other conscientious convictions of parents and
their children must be respected under the First Amendment, governments do not have a right, on the one hand,
to mandate the education of all children, and then, on the
other hand, to discriminate financially against those tax-
paying citizens who choose religiously qualified schools for
their children's education.[21]

Justice does require discrimination in some cases in the
funding of education. For example, handicapped or learn-
ing-disabled children may require a larger proportionate
expenditure if they are to receive the same level of schooling. High school education typically costs more than elementary education, so a greater proportionate investment
can be justified there. But beyond these and similar bases
for proportional discrimination, there can be no justification for discrimination on the basis of skin color, religion,
or the diverse pedagogical methods and philosophies of
schools freely chosen by parents and nonminor young
people.[22]

The way this approach deals with the First Amendment should be clearly evident by now. The First Amendment should be interpreted to require the protection of citizens' freedom to exercise their religious convictions without inhibition by government except where government must act to protect the lives, liberties, and properties of all citizens. If, because of conscience, some parents wish to educate their children in Catholic, or Protestant, or Jewish, or Muslim, or some other faith-guided school system, then the First Amendment's protection of their religious freedom must govern the distribution of public education dollars so as not to discriminate against them. Once we recognize that government need not own and operate all the agencies of education, then government's support of the schooling of its citizens in a variety of different school systems can be seen as completely compatible with First Amendment requirements.

The only danger to the First Amendment arises (as it now does, in fact) from government giving its financial and legal support to only one religious or ideological system of schools to the exclusion or disadvantage of others. Whether 5 percent or 95 percent of public funding goes to support religiously oriented schools, no infringement of the establishment clause exists as long as those schools are freely chosen by citizens without compulsion or special privileging of any of them by government. The so-called Blaine amendment is, in fact, an unjust attack on the very meaning of the First Amendment.

The question of racial, cultural, and gender discrimination is also met by means of the same pluriform openness to educational choice. As long as no child is excluded from equal educational opportunity, and equitable funding follows every child to the school of choice, then government need only watch to protect the pluriform openness of the public terrain. There is no reason, for example, why exclusively boys' or exclusively girls' schools may not be established, so long as children of the opposite sex are not kept from having other schools to choose from. As long as parents and educators are free to establish and to choose schools of every variety—Montessori schools; schools with classically oriented curricula; Asian, Latin, European, or other culturally unique schools; religiously distinct schools—then no one suffers discrimination simply because different schools have different degrees of uniqueness. Only when some children have no option, should the government take additional action—out of obligation to secure the equal opportunity of its citizens—to help those children find an acceptable school. But the government's action at that point should be to encourage the opening of yet further opportunity, not to close down the existing diversity in order to force some kind of homogeneous, public conformity.

Certain public, legal requirements binding on all parents and schools will remain perfectly legitimate in a pluriform system of schools. For the sake of civic well-being and fairness toward every citizen, there is no reason why governments should not require a certain level of competence in English from children at different age levels, or a certain level of competence in basic civic knowledge, and so forth. But these public mandates laid on all parents alike can be met by any number of means—in schools, at home, or by special tutoring agencies. Public-legal mandates by government designed to protect and enhance the public welfare need to be distinguished clearly from the right to own and operate educational agencies. The former does not grant a right of control over, or discrimination among, the latter. Basic language and math skills, civic knowledge, and other educational achievements have been nurtured by Catholic, Jewish, Protestant, and other nongovernment schools for more than two centuries. They can continue to be nurtured in a wide variety of schools equitably supported by public funds.

A pluriform system is also able to do justice to educators—to the wide variety of people who are competent to establish and serve in agencies of education such as schools, tutoring programs, and so forth. There is no constitutional or other reason of justice why government should be allowed to privilege its own schools to the disadvantage of other schools run by churches, parent associations, and independent educators. Once the distinction between state and society is made; once the distinction between school and government is accepted; then the ability of government to treat all schools fairly becomes possible. Of course, parents and guardians who will be responsible for choosing schools for their children need to be able to count on adequate and truthful information about the schools of choice. Government may need to establish new truth-in-advertising measures, and it may want to create better means of informing all families with school-age children about the variety of schools in their area. But all of these measures that have to do with government protection of both citizens and the public space in which schooling occurs are measures that should presuppose the independence of families and schools as well as the right of parents to choose schools for their children without any financial or legal discrimination against them.

Conclusion

s we complete the writing of this book, the United States Supreme Court is hearing oral arguments on two more cases dealing with religion and the schools (February 24, 1993). Beyond the walls of the Supreme Court Building, citizens in dozens of cities and states across the country are grappling with proposals for school reform. From New York City and Baltimore to Kansas City and Milwaukee, from Pennsylvania and Michigan to Washington and California, parents, educators, legislators, and judges are contending with one another over the future of education. In many of those cities and states, movements are growing in support of voucher programs that will allow parents to choose from among a greater number of schools for their children.[1]

Everywhere the issues are the same: how to improve learning for all children, especially for those who are poor and have little or no choice about the highly inadequate schools many of them now attend. Is it possible, some are asking, for citizens to share a common commitment to education and at the same time to agree to make room for the pursuit of learning in different religious, cultural, and pedagogical settings? Is there a fair and equitable way to give all parents the opportunity to choose from among a variety of schools for their children?

The arguments of the preceding chapters have a direct bearing both on the cases that keep coming before the Supreme Court and on the political controversies over school reform that are stirring around the country.

The Supreme Court and the Constitution

The most important school case before the Supreme Court in its 1992–93 term—*Zobrest* v. *Catalina Foothills School District* (Arizona)—concerned a deaf high school student, Jim Zobrest, who benefited from a federal law requiring states to help disabled children get an education. He benefited, that is, until he moved from a public school to a local Catholic school. At that point Arizona's attorney general, backing up the school district, judged that the U.S. Constitution forbids government aid to religion and that the state, therefore, could no longer fund the services of Zobrest's sign-language interpreter. Remarkably, the Arizona officials who made this judgment believed that if Jim Zobrest had chosen a private school that made no religious claims, the Constitution would have permitted the continuation of special aid.[2] Thus, discrimination in this instance was clearly due to Zobrest's decision to attend a self-professed religious school and not simply because he left a government-controlled school.

Quite in contrast to the judgment of the Arizona officials, we believe that the U.S. Constitution yields a different interpretation—one that we hope the Supreme Court itself will offer in the *Zobrest* case. On First Amendment grounds we believe that government's general support for education should not be religiously discriminatory. Citizens should not have to compromise their religious convictions in order to benefit from a public service paid for by general taxation. If, as in the Arizona case, government denies educational services to a student who decides to attend a self-professed religious school, the government is, from our point of view, overtly violating the religious freedom of that student. According to William Bentley Ball, the attorney who argued Zobrest's case before the Supreme Court, the primary effect of the federal disabilities law on Jim Zobrest, no matter what school he attended, was to advance his education, not to advance one religion over another.[3] To deny him a general educational benefit because he chose to follow his conscience is to violate his religious freedom.

We believe, with William Ball, that the Supreme Court should reverse the lower court's decision in *Zobrest* not simply in order to restore the young man's religious freedom but also in order to expose the deeper error underlying that act of discrimination. The deeper mistake of Arizona officials—as it has been of many Supreme Court decisions—has been to assume that government-run schools (and many private schools making no religious claims) are themselves, in fact, religiously neutral. As both Johnson and Baer have shown, schooling by its very nature cannot be religiously neutral. Therefore, the actual effect of the Arizona decision, if it were to be upheld as constitutional, would be to give constitutional privilege to the philosophy and curricular views of the schools that government does choose to fund. The First Amendment consequence, in other words, would be the same as a religious *establishment*—that is, to provide government backing to one set of non-neutral dogmas while discriminating against others.

If our federal and state governments did not fund education at all, or if schooling were not required of all children, then the legal issues might appear in a different light. But that is not the situation in the United States. Both the general requirement of schooling and the taxation to support that schooling are compelled by government. Consider for a moment the law under which Jim Zobrest received the help of an interpreter. The federal government's 1991 Education of the Handicapped Act was enacted to ensure that *no* child would be denied an education because of a handicap. The greatest handicap for Jim Zobrest, however, turned out to be his religious convictions rather than his deafness. In effect, the state government, relying on a long-standing but (in our view) faulty interpretation of the Constitution, defied the plain purpose of the federal statute. Instead of allowing special funding to go to this physically handicapped student as intended by the law, the state threw up the additional handicap of a religious test. Only if the young man acted in a way that met a religious test (in this case, that he *not* attend a self-professed religious school), would the government allow him to receive the services offered by the federal government.

What the Supreme Court needs to do now is to clarify unambiguously the First Amendment foundation that ought to govern educational policymaking. Just as the federal government tried to overcome the physical handicap of a deaf student by making sure that the extra expense of a sign-language interpreter would not keep him from getting an education, so, we believe, the Supreme Court ought to rule that no student should suffer from a religious handicap that would keep him or her from receiving a free education. Government support of education, whether by way of general funding for ordinary schooling or special funding for handicapped students, should go to every eligible student without religious discrimination—regardless of whether a student's choice of school is based on Christian, Jewish, Muslim, or secularist convictions. Government-run schools, in other words, should not be allowed to monopolize public funding by virtue of the specious argument that such schools are truly neutral with respect to religion and that the First Amendment really does disqualify professedly religious schools from receiving public funding.

Interestingly, a reporter for *The Washington Post* inadvertently provided support for our argument when commenting on another case that the Supreme Court took up during its 1992–93 term. *Lamb's Chapel* v. *Center Moriches Union Free School District* is a New York case that concerns a church's right to use public school premises during nonschool hours. Many other organizations were permitted to use the facilities, but in the case of Lamb's Chapel, the judgment was negative. The state's case against the church was grounded in the unexamined prejudice that religion is such a *private* matter than any activities sponsored by a church could not meet the "public forum" test applied to other organizations. Joan Biskupic, reporting for the *Post* on the *Lamb's Chapel* case, concluded her article with this paragraph:

> Two earlier court cases might guide the [Supreme Court] justices. In the 1990 *Westside Community Schools* v. *Mergens*, the court said student religious groups may meet in public high schools on the same basis as other extracurricular clubs. In the 1981 *Widmar* v. *Vincent*, the justices let religious groups meet on college campuses. The upshot has been that, once a school allows wide access for various social and civic groups, it may not discriminate against others based on their religious, philosophical or political viewpoints.[4]

Biskupic's concluding sentence points the way to sound reasoning not only for the *Lamb's Chapel* case but also for nondiscrimination in schooling generally. We can state it this way: once government has decided to require, and to collect taxes for, the education of all children, government should not be allowed to discriminate against any of those children "based on their religious, philosophical, or political viewpoints." Since it is impossible to educate all children in a religiously or philosophically neutral fashion, we believe that the best way for government to offer nondiscriminatory education to a diverse public is to allow all parents, with equitable support of public funding, to choose schools for their children without suffering discrimination because of their religious, philosophical, or political viewpoints.

Just as it would be discriminatory if the state of New York allowed only religious groups to use public school facilities, so it is discriminatory for it to exclude only those that are self-professedly religious. Just as it would be unconstitutional for the government to fund only Presbyterian or Catholic schools and not Jewish or secular schools, so it is unconstitutional for it to fund only government-run schools and to discriminate against other schools that parents may choose in order to fulfill the public-legal requirement that their children receive an education.

The only way that government could be consistent in discriminating financially against nongovernment schools would be if it actually outlawed all schools other than its own. Then it would, in effect, by saying that the *only* way citizens may fulfill the public mandate of schooling is to send their children to schools established and run by government. Historically, however, state and federal governments in America have never been granted the constitutional right to enforce such a restriction.[5] Governments have allowed parents who wish to educate their children in nongovernment schools to do so. Independent schools have been recognized as a legitimate means by which parents may fulfill the *public-legal* mandate to educate their children.

However, despite the ostensible freedom to choose schools, discriminatory public funding laws have remained in dispute for the past 150 years. How can laws be fair and just that require parents to educate their children and to pay taxes for that education but which also demand that parents send their children only to government-run schools in order to benefit from the educational services funded by their public tax dollars? It is one thing to say that parents are free to exercise choice in educating their children. It is quite another thing for government to withhold educational funding from the children of those parents who feel conscience-bound to choose an independent school.

Jim Zobrest suffered a violation of his First Amendment right of religious freedom by being denied public educational benefits simply because of his religious convictions. The consequence of the Arizona decision that denied him those benefits was to establish a religious test for what should be a universal public benefit for handicapped students. That also amounts to a violation of the establishment clause of the First Amendment.

In Cities and States across America

Depending on whether the U.S. Supreme Court reinterprets the Constitution along the lines we have proposed, a number of changes might be implemented rather quickly in the laws that govern educational funding. Many cities and states are straining to find new ways to improve schooling—especially for those trapped in the worst schools.

Maryland's Democratic Governor William Donald Schaefer, for example, put before his state's 1993 legislature a proposal for a pilot project that would give a voucher of $2,900 to each of 200 school children from poor families in Baltimore. The voucher could be used at any school, including self-professed religious schools.[6] The model behind Schaefer's proposal is Milwaukee's pilot project initiated and promoted by Wisconsin State Rep. Polly Williams, another Democrat who believes that radical changes in education are necessary.[7] Schaefer wants to go beyond the Milwaukee experiment, which limits its public funding to so-called nonsectarian independent schools.

The argument of this book clearly backs Schaefer's proposal, insisting that a state should be free to fund a diversity of educational choices by parents who are, after all, responsible for rearing their children. The contemporary crisis of American schools is not caused by religious diversity. Many Catholic and other self-professed religious schools in the inner cities and elsewhere are more integrated, less costly, more harmonious, and more advanced educationally than their government-run counterparts. In making his proposal, Schaefer said that the time has come for public schools to face competition: "Unfortunately, with the public schools, status quo and no change seem to be the buzzwords."[8] Not only do we agree with the governor that education today requires experimentation and competition; we also believe that schooling needs to be released from the bondage of restrictive interpretations of the First Amendment—interpretations that have in one way or another enforced religious discrimination for the past 150 years.

Certainly many of those who now have a controlling interest in government-run schools want to protect their monopoly over public education dollars. The reaction from the Maryland State Teachers Association to Schaefer's proposed pilot project in Baltimore, for example, was one of outright opposition. "The teachers union is rallying its troops against the voucher program, saying that even a pilot effort would give private schools a foothold in future state budget deliberations, enabling them to compete for money the public schools would otherwise receive."[9] Does this opposition from the teachers union spring from an overriding concern to improve schooling for poor children, or from a better argument about how to overcome the racial discrimination that persists in our cities, or from the deep desire to do greater justice to conscientious parents who want to find the best education for their children? No. The overriding concern of the teachers union appears to be a desire to maintain control of public funding for government-run schools despite the fact that many of those schools are failing the children who are supposed to benefit from a free education. Maryland legislator Howard P. Rawlings, a Democrat from Baltimore who fully supports the voucher proposal, says, "I think a voucher program targeted to low-income, working-class families would provide them with the same education options middle-class and upper middle-class families have. That is blatantly fair."[10]

Not only would the Baltimore experiment be fair; it is what we should expect from a government that is funding education for the benefit of all students. The whole point of tax-supported free education is supposed to be that every child, regardless of race and economic background, should have the same opportunity to receive a good education so that each will be able to participate in society on a fair and equitable basis. Why should poor people be denied a choice of schools simply because they are poor? Why should schools, which want to educate children regardless of their race or economic background, be denied the opportunity to do so simply because they are self-professedly religious in character? Why should parents with one kind of religious conviction about schooling be denied equal public funding for the education of their children while parents with a different view of education are given full funding? The only good answer to each of these questions is: it should not be so.

Looking back from our contemporary vantage point, we can see that the Blaine amendment, which remains ensconced in many state constitutions, represents a blatant violation of the First Amendment's guarantee of religious freedom. The effort being made today to improve educational quality and fairness for all will be enhanced by allowing parents and students to make their own choices from among a diversity of school systems, both independent and government-run.[11] In the final analysis, we believe that the Constitution's First Amendment requires the protection of religious freedom when parents and students choose schools. Not until the government-school monopoly over public funding is broken will we have the assurance that government is not establishing a religion or a religiously equivalent viewpoint in public schooling. Not until religious freedom is fully respected in the education of all children will the school-choice controversy find a fair and equitable resolution.

Notes

Introduction

1. John Courtney Murray, "A Common Enemy, a Common Cause," *First Things* (October 1992), p. 35.

2. Ibid., p. 36.

3. Ibid. See also Richard A. Baer, Jr., "The Supreme Court's Discriminatory Use of the Term 'Sectarian'," *Journal of Law and Politics* (Spring 1990), pp. 449–68.

Chapter 1: *"Strict Neutrality" and Our Monopoly System*

1. Here and elsewhere in this essay I deliberately use the term "government public school" rather than simply "public school." This is because private or independent schools serve a public purpose in roughly the same way as do public schools. Also, because poor people typically cannot afford housing in neighborhoods with the best public schools, many "public" schools are not really open to the general public. Overall, social, economic, and racial integration in independent schools compares favorably with that in government public schools. See James S. Coleman, Thomas Hoffer, and Sally Kilgore, *High School Achievement: Public, Catholic, and Private Schools Compared* (New York: Basic Books, 1982), pp. 28–71.

2. See especially Louis Raths, Merrill Harmin, and Sidney B. Simon, *Values and Teaching* (Columbus, Ohio: Charles E. Merrill, 1966; 2d ed. 1978); Sidney B. Simon, Leland W. Howe, and Howard Kirschenbaum, *Values Clarification* (New York: Hart, 1972; rev. ed., 1978); Howard Kirschenbaum and Sidney Simon, *Readings in Values Clarification* (Minneapolis: Winston Press, 1973).

3. Given the extraordinary attentiveness the U.S. Supreme Court has displayed to the religious sensitivities of Jews, atheists, and others who might be offended by overtly Christian elements in school curricula, it is puzzling that courts have remained almost totally insensitive to complaints from Christian parents that the religious beliefs of their chil-

dren were being belittled and undermined by methods like Values Clarification or the home economic textbooks that were disputed in *Smith v. Board of School Commissioners of Mobile County*, 655 F.Supp. 939 (S.D.Ala. 1987). See *Abington School District v. Schempp*, 374 U.S. at 208, 209. At 305 (Justice Goldberg with Justice Harlan, concurring) we read: "The fullest realization of true religious liberty requires that government neither engage in nor compel religious practices, that it effect no favoritism among sects or between religion and nonreligion, and that it work deterrence of no religious belief."

4. The following are examples of scores of articles that have appeared over the past two decades: William J. Bennett and Edwin J. Delattre, "Moral Education in the Schools, *Public Interest*, 50 (Winter 1978), pp. 81–98; Alan L. Lockwood, "Values Education and the Right to Privacy," *Journal of Moral Education*, vol. 7, no. 1 (1977), pp. 9–26; John S. Stewart, "Clarifying Values Clarification: A Critique," *Phi Delta Kappan*, vol. 56, no. 10 (1975), pp. 684–88; Richard A. Baer, Jr., "Values Clarification as Indoctrination," *Educational Forum*, vol. 41, no. 2 (1977), pp. 155–65; idem, "Teaching Values in the Schools: Clarification or Indoctrination?" *Principal*, vol. 61, no. 3 (January 1982), pp. 17–21, 36.

5. For an especially flagrant violation of academic protocol, see Sidney Simon, "Sidney Simon's Response," *Phi Delta Kappan*, vol. 41, no. 10 (1975) p. 682. Written in response to a fair, and even generous, critique of Values Clarification by John S. Stewart, Simon writes (among other things):

> If John Stewart had been less petulant and cranky, I might be willing to listen to him, but as it is, I don't trust him. I don't think he is really concerned with making this life better for teachers and children.
>
> His real interest seems to be with dazzling his academic, ivory tower peer group. I find that a useless recreation and reactive rather than directive. It is like the kid in the neighborhood who can't play baseball and so stands two streets away mumbling deprecations out of earshot at the kids who are having a marvelous, joyful funfilled ball game.
>
> On the other hand, perhaps he is envious about the many ways we in the values clarification movement have been useful to thousands of teachers. Our popularity makes some stuffy people rage for our jugular veins. More likely it is simply his propensity for splitting hairs.
>
> Well, while he mouths his philosophical pretensions, I will continue to devote my own energies to inventing more and more creative ways for people to look at their lives and for making this world better for kids who have to go to school.

6. See Martin Eger, "The Conflict in Moral Education: An Informal Case Study," *Public Interest* 63 (Spring 1981), pp. 62–80.

7. See Francis Baynor Parnell, *Homemaking Skills for Everyday Living* (South Holland, Ill.: Goodheart-Wilcox, 1984), pp. 14, 16, 80; Verdene Ryder, *Contemporary Living* (South Holland, Ill.: Goodheart-Wilcox, 1984), pp. 49, 97; Helen McGinley, *Caring, Deciding, and Growing* (Lexington, Mass.: Ginn, 1981), p. 5; Joan Kelly and Eddye Eubanks, *Today's Teen* (Peoria, Ill.: Charles A. Bennett, 1981), p. 26; Martha Davis Dunn and M. Yvonne Peeler, *Living, Learning and Caring* (Lexington, Mass.: Ginn, 1984), p. 5. Cf. *Abington School District v. Schempp*, 374 U.S. 218: "We agree of course that the State may not establish a 'religion of secularism' in the sense of affirmatively opposing or showing hostility to religion." Given the zeal with which the courts have smoked out every trace of tradi-

tional religion in government public school curricula and practices, it is truly remarkable that they have never prohibited materials like Values Clarification from being used in these schools. In *Smith* v. *Board of School Commissioners of Mobile County*, 827 F.2d 684 (11th Cir. 1987) the Eleventh Circuit Court of Appeals brushed aside many hours of expert testimony with superficial and largely irrelevant comments, concluding that the judgment of the district court that the challenged textbooks "advanced secular humanism and inhibited theistic religion . . . [was] in error." Even admitting that Judge Brevard Hand's District Court decision was not well crafted, the Eleventh Circuit Court conclusion—"Nor do these textbooks evidence an attitude antagonistic to theistic belief"—is so totally mistaken that it must be described as utterly incompetent. How these judges could have reached such a conclusion in light of the telling evidence and well-developed philosophical arguments of the plaintiff's witnesses is almost beyond belief.

8. See Ryder, *Contemporary Living*; McGinley, *Caring, Deciding, and Growing*.

9. One of the ironies related to the marketplace-of-ideas model for government public schools is the long line of cases that try to fine-tune the nature of free speech in these schools while almost totally overlooking the fact that the basic structure of the school is coercive of people's consciences, especially of those families who cannot afford alternative independent schools for their children. The Supreme Court argues that government "may not grant the use of a forum to people whose views it finds acceptable, but deny use to those wishing to express less favored or more controversial views." (*Tinker* v. *Des Moines*, 408 U.S. 92 at 96 [1972]). *Tinker* takes what in some ways is a very liberal view regarding students' First Amendment freedom of speech rights, but it quite overlooks the far deeper government censorship involved in including and excluding ideas and values from school curricula, deciding what subjects will and will not be taught. Even government certification of teachers is through and through an anti-marketplace-of-ideas strategy. Just think how offensive it would be to have government certification of newspapers and periodicals. See also *Police Department of Chicago* v. *Mosley*, 408 U.S. 92 at 96 (1972), a case that deals with picketing or demonstrating on a public way near a public school building: "[Government] may not select which issues are worth discussing or debating in public facilities." See Richard A. Baer, Jr., "Public Education as 'Brutal Censorship,'" *This World*, no. 22 (Summer 1988), pp. 110–15.

10. *Schempp*, 374 U.S. 225: "Nothing we have said here indicates that such study of the Bible or of religion, when presented objectively as part of a secular program of education, may not be effected consistently with the First Amendment."

11. See discussion in *McCollum* v. *Board of Education*, 333 U.S. 203 at 236 and *Schempp*, 374 U.S. at 300.

12. I have heard secular educators reject such a compromise solution with the argument that students are always free to pray silently on their own if they so choose. But this response overlooks the fact that it is difficult to pray when people all around are talking, and to break off a conversation in progress at lunchtime is decidedly awkward. We would not think of saying to someone at a chamber music concert, "Don't get upset that people are talking and shuffling around the concert hall. If you really want to hear the music you can concentrate a bit harder."

13. To take a particular case of current moral inquiry, I find a kind of quaint parochialness in the cavalier way in which Peter Singer, Tom Regan, and other philosophers concerned with animal rights brush aside religious and theological views of the uniqueness of human beings. They seem utterly oblivious to the fact that their own initial assumptions about morality and the nature of reality just as clearly go beyond pure logic or tech-

nical reason or rationality per se as do the starting points of, say, Christian theologians. The terms "rational," "rationality," "reason," and "reasonable" function in much contemporary discussion in an epistemologically imperialistic fashion. Their use by many secularists is similar to their use of the term "nonsectarian," and it is often no more justifiable philosophically than was Jefferson's biased habit of referring to the religious views of orthodox Christians as "sectarian." Cf. Richard A. Baer, Jr., "The Supreme Court's Discriminatory Use of the Term 'Sectarian,'" *Journal of Law and Politics*, vol. 6, no. 3 (Spring 1990), pp. 449–68. See also Peter Singer, *Animal Liberation* (New York: New York Review, 2d ed., 1990), pp. 270–71, n. 14; Tom Regan and Peter Singer, *Animal Rights and Human Obligations* (Englewood Cliffs, N.J.: Prentice Hall, 2d ed. 1989), pp. 111–12. For an interpretation similar in some respects to my own, see Keith Tester, *Animals and Society: The Humanity of Animal Rights* (New York: Routledge, 1991).

14. See Thomas A. Spragens, Jr., *The Irony of Liberal Reason* (Chicago: University of Chicago Press, 1981), pp. 311–95; Richard J. Bernstein, ed., *Habermas and Modernity* (Cambridge, Mass.: MIT, 1985), "Introduction," pp. 1–8; Hilary Putnam, *Reason, Truth and History* (New York: Cambridge University Press, 1981), pp. 174–216; Alasdair MacIntyre, *Whose Justice, Which Rationality?* (Notre Dame, Ind.: University of Notre Dame Press, 1988), pp. 1–11, 326–403; Jeffrey Stout, *Ethics after Babel* (Boston: Beacon, 1988), pp. 1–32, 220–65.

15. Richard A. Baer, Jr., "The Supreme Court's Discriminatory Use of the Term 'Sectarian,'" *Journal of Law and Politics*, vol. 6, no. 3 (Spring 1990), p. 452.

16. Cf. the phrase "a brooding and pervasive devotion to the secular and a passive, or even active, hostility to the religious" in *Schempp*, 374 U.S. at 306 (Justice Goldberg joined by Justice Harlan, concurring). Many Christian and Jewish parents today view government public school curricula in precisely such terms.

17. John Dewey, *A Common Faith* (New Haven: Yale University Press, 1934), p. 87.

18. John Dewey, *Characters and Events: Popular Essays in Social and Political Philosophy*, ed. Joseph Ratner (New York: Henry Holt, 1929), 2:514.

19. Quoted in Robert E. Webber, *Secular Humanism: Threat and Challenge*, p. 29. See Y. H. Kirkorian, *Naturalism and the Human Spirit* (New York: Columbia University Press, 1944), p. 382.

20. Quoted in Homer Duncan, *The Religion of Secular Humanism and the Public Schools* (Lubbock, Tex.: MC International, n.d.), pp. 5–25. See Charles Francis Potter, *Humanism: A New Religion* (New York: Simon and Schuster, 1930).

21. Potter, *Humanism*, p. 3.

22. The idea that humanism or secularism can function as a religion can also be found in U.S. Supreme Court cases. See *Torcaso v. Watkins*, 367 U.S. 488 at 495 in footnote: "Among religions in this country which do not teach what would generally be considered a belief in the existence of God are Buddhism, Taoism, Ethical Culture, Secular Humanism, and others." See also *Schempp*, 374 U.S. 203 at 313, where Justice Stewart, dissenting, refers to "a religion of secularism." See James Davison Hunter, *Culture Wars: The Struggle to Define America* (New York: Basic Books, 1991), p. 131 for a discussion of Emile Durkheim's view of the sacred. Hunter writes: "For Durkheim, the sacred was not necessarily embodied in a divine or supernatural being, the sacred could be anything that was viewed as 'set apart' and 'exalted'; anything that provided the life-orienting principles of individuals and the larger community."

23. *United States v. Seeger*, 380 U.S. 163.

24. *Welsh v. United States*, 398 U.S. 333.

25. See *Seeger* at 182 where the Court quotes approvingly a passage from "the recent Ecumenical Council": "Men expect from the various religions answers to the riddles of the human condition: What is man? What is the meaning and purpose of our lives? What is the moral good and what is sin? What are death, judgment, and retribution after death?" These concerns are very close to what I call "the Big Questions," and methods like Values Clarification or some of the sex education curricula used in government public schools clearly deal with a number of these issues. These curricula make sweeping assumptions (almost never explicitly discussed or debated) about the meaning and purpose of life, and the very fact that they do not talk about judgment and retribution after death is significant, for they strongly imply that human beings are not responsible to any transcendent being such as the God of the Jewish and Christian Scriptures. See references in n. 4 above. Because of its inadequate framework for understanding how the secular is related to the religious, the Court not infrequently ends up distorting past and present cultural reality in a way that is demeaning to religious Americans and historically preposterous. Cf. *Lynch v. Donnelly,* 465 U.S. 668 at 716: "for despite its religious antecedents, the current practice of celebrating Thanksgiving is unquestionably secular and patriotic." Or cf. 717, where we are told that the message of religious art at the National Gallery, presidential references to God during inaugural addresses, and the like are "dominantly secular." Such a claim is like a white American saying that whites ought to accept blacks because they are "basically just like we are."

26. Cf. *Shelton v. Tucker,* 364 U.S. 479, at 488 (1960), where the Court held that "even though the governmental purpose be legitimate and substantial, that purpose cannot be pursued by means that broadly stifle fundamental personal liberties when the end can be more narrowly achieved." I agree that the state has a compelling interest in education, but I do not see that it has any compelling interest in operating schools and universities itself. Insofar as government schools inevitably trample on people's rights of conscience, it would be constitutionally preferable for schools to be independently operated.

27. This statement may appear puzzling in light of my earlier arguments, for my point was that all schools are basically "religious." If my analysis is correct, then public support of nongovernment, traditionally religious schools is every bit as legitimate constitutionally as public support of our present system of secular (but in actuality, religious) public schools.

Chapter 2: *The "Blaine Amendment" in State Constitutions*

1. Mann's declaration is reprinted in Anson P. Stokes, *Church and State in the United States* (New York: Harper, 1950), 2:57.

2. 4 *Cong. Rec.* 175 (1875).

3. The text of the Blaine amendment is reprinted in Conrad H. Moehlman, *The American Constitutions and Religion: Religious References in the Charters of the Thirteen Colonies and the Constitutions of the Forty-Eight States* (Berne, Ind.: Private Publication, 1938), p. 17.

4. *Cong. Rec.* 180, 243 app., 5562–95 (1876).

5. Enabling Act. ch. 180, §4, 25 Stat. 676–77 (1889).

6. Washington Constitution, art. IX, §1.

7. T. Stiles, "The Constitution of the State and Its Effect upon Public Interests," 4 *Washington Historical Quarterly* 281, 284 (1913).

8. *Morning Oregonian*, July 4, 1889, at 11, col. 1.

9. *Washington Constitution*, art. I, §11.

10. *Witters v. Commission for the Blind*, 102 Wn.2d 624, 689 P.2d 53 (1984).

11. *Witters v. Washington Dept. of Services for the Blind*, 474 U.S. 481 (1986).

12. *Witters v. Commission for the Blind*, 112 Wn.2d 363, 771 P.2d 1119 (1989).

13. *Id.* at 368.

14. *Weiss v. Bruno*, 82 Wn.2d 199, 509 P.2d 973 (1973).

15. *Witters*, 112 Wn.2d at 368.

16. *Id.* at 369.

Chapter 3: *School Vouchers and the United States Constitution*

1. See Peter Berger, *The Capitalist Revolution* (New York: Basic Books, 1986), for the classic discussion of the "knowledge class" and its self-interested preference for state coercion over private initiative.

2. *Abington School District v. Schempp*, 374 U.S. 203 (1963); *Engel v. Vitale*, 370 U.S. 421 (1963).

3. For background information on the Washington clause and its relationship to similar provisions in other states, see Robert F. Utter and Edward J. Larson, "Church and State on the Frontier: The History of the Establishment Clauses in the Washington State Constitution," 15 *Hastings Constitutional Law Quarterly* 451 (1988).

4. *Witters v. Washington Dept. of Services for the Blind*, 102 Wash.2d 624, 689 P.2d 53 (1984).

5. *Lemon v. Kurtzman*, 403 U.S. 602, 612–13 (1971).

6. See *Marsh v. Chambers*, 463 U.S. 783 (1983), in which a divided Supreme Court upheld the custom of opening legislative sessions with prayer because of its long historical acceptance. Compare *Abington School District v. Schempp*, 374 U.S. 201, 226 (1963), where the Court referred in passing to "a situation such as military service, where the Government regulates the temporal and geographic environment of individuals to a point that, unless it permits voluntary religious services to be conducted with the use of government facilities, military personnel would be unable to engage in the practice of their faiths."

7. *Witters v. Washington Dept. of Services for the Blind*, 474 U.S. 481 (1986).

8. See *Committee for Public Education v. Nyquist*, 413 U.S. 756 (1973).

9. *Witters*, 474, U.S. at 491 (opinion of Justice Powell).

10. For example, Justices Kennedy and Scalia provided an important indication of their approach to religious establishment claims in a concurring opinion in *Bowen v. Kendrick*, 108 S.Ct. 2562, (1988). They noted that previous decisions had held that "a statute which provides for exclusive or disproportionate funding to pervasively sectarian institutions may impermissibly advance religion and as such be invalid on its face." Nonetheless, where "a statute provides that the benefits of a program are to be distributed in a neutral fashion to religious and non-religious applicants alike, and the program withstands a facial challenge, it is not unconstitutional as applied solely by reason of the religious character of a specific recipient." See *Bowen v. Kendrick*, 487 U.S. 589, 624 (1988) (concurring opinion of Justice Kennedy, joined by Justice Scalia).

11. *Witters* v. *State Department for the Blind*, 112 Wash.2d 363, 771 P.2d 1119, cert. denied, 493 U.S. 850 (1989).

12. Cf. *Employment Division, Department of Human Resources of Oregon* v. *Smith*, 494 U.S. 872 (1990).

13. See *Widmar* v. *Vincent*, 454 U.S. 263 (1981). While this book was in press, the Supreme Court decided *Zobrest* v. *Catalina Foothills School District*, 61 U.S. Law Week 4641 (June 18, 1993). The majority opinion by Chief Justice Rehnquist held that the establishment clause does not bar a school district from providing a sign-language interpreter to a deaf student attending a Roman Catholic high school. The holding in *Zobrest* generally supports the analysis in this chapter, but changes in the membership of the Supreme Court make it difficult to predict future decisions.

Chapter 4: *Educational Freedom with Justice*

1. For the historical background, see Rockne M. McCarthy, James W. Skillen, and William A. Harper, *Disestablishment a Second Time: Genuine Pluralism for American Schools* (Grand Rapids: Eerdmans, 1982), pp. 30–51; Charles L. Glenn, Jr., *The Myth of the Common School* (Amherst: University of Massachusetts Press, 1988), pp. 86–178; James W. Skillen, "Thomas Jefferson and the Religious Character of Education," *Religion and Public Education*, vol. 14 (Winter 1987), pp. 379–84; James B. Conant, *Thomas Jefferson and the Development of American Public Education* (Los Angeles: University of California Press, 1970); David Little, "Thomas Jefferson's Religious Views and Their Influence on the Supreme Court's Interpretation of the First Amendment," *Catholic University Law Review*, vol. 56 (1976), pp. 56ff.; David Little, "The Origins of Perplexity: Civil Religion and Moral Belief in the Thought of Thomas Jefferson," in Russell E. Richey and Donald G. Jones, eds., *American Civil Religion* (New York: Harper and Row, 1974), pp. 185–210; Benjamin Rush, "Thoughts upon the Mode of Education Proper in a Republic," in Fredrick Rudolph, ed., *Essays on Education in the Early Republic* (Cambridge: Harvard University Press, 1965), pp. 5–17; Lawrence Cremin, ed., *The Republic and the School: Horace Mann on the Education of Free Men* (New York: Teachers College Press, 1957); Jonathan Messerli, *Horace Mann: A Biography* (New York: Knopf, 1972).

2. Diane Ravitch, *The Great School Wars: New York City, 1805–1973* (New York: Basic Books, 1974), pp. 251ff.

3. Glenn, *Myth of the Common School*, pp. 158–78; Raymond B. Culver, *Horace Mann and Religion in the Massachusetts Public Schools* (New Haven: Yale University Press, 1929); Neil G. McCluskey, *Public Schools and Moral Education: The Influence of Horace Mann, William Torrey Harris, and John Dewey* (New York: Columbia University Press, 1958).

4. McCarthy, Skillen, and Harper, *Disestablishment a Second Time*, pp. 52–90; Rocke M. McCarthy, "Public Schools and Public Justice: The Past, the Present, and the Future," in Richard John Neuhaus, ed., *Democracy and the Renewal of Public Education* (Grand Rapids: Eerdmans, 1987), pp. 57–75; Michael B. Katz, *Class, Bureaucracy, and Schools: The Illusion of Educational Change in America* (New York: Praeger, 1975), pp. 56–104. Katz says that if our present bureaucratic system of education was an inevitability, those who lived at the time of its creation certainly did not believe that to be true. In the first half of the nineteenth century there were four different models or proposals for organizing schools. The government-run, bureaucratic model simply won the day and by 1880 "American education had acquired its fundamental structural characteristics," which

have not altered since (p. xvii). On twentieth-century developments, see Laurence Ian-naccone, "Changing Political Patterns and Governmental Regulations," in Robert B. Ever-hart, ed., *The Public School Monopoly* (San Francisco: Pacific Institute for Public Policy Research, 1982), pp. 295–324.

5. See Ravitch, *Great School Wars,* pp. 33–76; Glenn, *Myth of the Common School,* pp. 196–206; Vincent Lannie, *Public Money and Parochial Education: Bishop Hughes, Gover-nor Seward, and the New York Controversy* (Cleveland: Case Western Reserve University Press, 1968); Stanley K. Schultz, *The Culture Factory: Boston Public Schools, 1789–1860* (New York: Oxford University Press, 1973).

6. See Edward G. Hartmann, *The Movement to Americanize the Immigrant* (New York: Columbia University Press, 1948); Ray Allen Billington, *The Protestant Crusade, 1800–1860: A Study of the Origins of American Nativism* (Chicago: Quadrangle Paper-backs, 1964 [1938]; Herman Eschenbacher, "Education and Social Unity in the Ante-bel-lum Period," *Harvard Educational Review,* vol. 30 (Spring 1960); C. H. Edson, "School-ing for Work and Working at School: Perspectives on Immigrant and Working-Class Education in Urban America, 1880–1920," in Everhart, ed., *Public School Monopoly,* pp. 145–87; Charles L. Glenn, Jr., "'Molding' Citizens," in Neuhaus, ed., *Democracy and the Renewal of Public Education,* pp. 25–56; and Glenn, *Myth of the Common School,* pp. 73–84.

7. The issue of whether "public" schools are, or can be, religiously and ideologically neutral arises at this point. The claim of neutrality is made by those who assume that "nonsectarian" means "neutral." But all the evidence points to the impossibility of neu-trality in any form of education, as Richard Baer argues in the first chapter. See also Richard A. Baer, Jr., "American Public Education and the Myth of Value Neutrality," in Neuhaus, ed., *Democracy and the Renewal of Public Education,* pp. 1–24; idem, "The Myth of Neu-trality," in Ken Sidey, ed., *The Blackboard Fumble* (Wheaton, Ill.: Victor Books, 1989); and idem, "The Supreme Court's Discriminatory Use of the Term 'Sectarian,'" *Journal of Law and Politics,* vol. 6 (Spring 1990), pp. 449–68.

8. See Ravitch, *Great School Wars,* pp. 251–378; Maurice R. Berube and Marilyn Git-tell, eds., *Confrontation at Ocean Hill-Brownsville* (New York: Praeger, 1969); Caroline Persell, *Education and Inequality* (New York: Free Press, 1977); Gary Orfield, *The Recon-struction of Southern Education: The Schools and the 1964 Civil Rights Act* (New York: Wiley-Interscience, 1969).

9. More extended, historical development of this argument can be found in James W. Skillen, "Religion and Education Policy: Where Do We Go from Here?" *The Journal of Law and Politics,* vol. 6 (Spring 1990), pp. 503–29; McCarthy, Skillen, and Harper, *Dis-establishment a Second Time,* pp. 15–72; Skillen, "Thomas Jefferson and the Religious Character of Education."

10. Katz, *Class, Bureaucracy, and Schools,* pp. 3–104; Glenn, *Myth of the Common School,* pp. 115–45, 219–35, 249–61; Lawrence Cremin, *American Education: The National Experience, 1783–1876* (New York: Harper and Row, 1980); Samuel Bowles and Herbert Gintis, *Schooling in Capitalist America* (New York: Basic Books, 1976), pp. 151–79.

11. The development of this argument will unfold below. See Skillen, "Religion and Education Policy."

12. For an introduction to the idea of political pluralism or pluriformity, see James W. Skillen and Rockne M. McCarthy, eds., *Political Order and the Plural Structure of Soci-ety* (Atlanta: Scholars Press, 1991), esp. "Introduction." For background on different approaches to the ordering of pluriform societies, see Kenneth McRae, ed., *Consociational Democracy: Political Accommodation in Segmented Societies* (Toronto: McClelland and

Stewart, 1974), particularly Jurg Steiner, "The Principles of Majority and Proportionality," pp. 98–106; Arend Lijphart, "Typologies of Democratic Systems," *Comparative Political Studies*, vol. 1 (1968), pp. 3–44; and James W. Skillen and Stanley W. Carlson-Thies, "Religion and Political Development in Nineteenth-Century Holland," *Publius*, vol. 12 (Summer 1982), pp. 43–64. With regard to schooling and the plural structure of society, see Charles L. Glenn, Jr., *Choice of Schools in Six Nations* (Washington, D.C.: U.S. Department of Education, 1989).

13. William Lee Miller, *The First Liberty: Religion and the American Republic* (New York: Knopf, 1986); James Davison Hunter and Os Guinness, eds., *Articles of Faith, Articles of Peace: The Religious Liberty Clauses and the American Public Philosophy* (Washington, D.C.: The Bookings Institution, 1990), pp. 17–39.

14. See the "Williamsburg Charter," and James Davison Hunter, "Religious Freedom and the Challenge of Modern Pluralism," in Hunter and Guinness, eds., *Articles of Faith, Articles of Peace*, pp. 125–45 and pp. 54–73, respectively.

15. See Rockne M. McCarthy, et al., *Society, State, and Schools: A Case for Structural and Confessional Pluralism* (Grand Rapids: Eerdmans, 1981), pp. 51–78; Lawrence M. Friedman, *A History of American Law* (New York: Simon and Schuster Touchstone Book, 1973), pp. 179–91, 428–40; John E. Coons, "Intellectual Liberty and the Schools," *Journal of Law, Ethics and Public Policy*, vol. 1 (1985), pp. 495–533; Maris A. Vinovskis, "American Institutions and the Study of Family Life in the Past," in John E. Jackson, ed., *Institutions in American Society: Essays in Market, Political, and Social Organizations* (Ann Arbor: University of Michigan Press, 1990), pp. 57–80; Amy Gutman, "Children, Paternalism and Education," *Philosophy and Public Affairs*, vol. 9 (1980), pp. 338ff.; William E. Nelson, *Americanization of the Common Law: The Impact of Legal Change on Massachusetts Society, 1760–1830* (Cambridge: Harvard University Press, 1975), pp. 101–16; Michael Gordon, ed., *The American Family in Social-Historical Perspective* (New York: St. Martin's Press, 1973); Theodore K. Rabb and Robert I. Rotberg, eds., *The Family in History: Interdisciplinary Essays* (New York: Harper Torchbooks, 1973). Several relevant court cases are cited in Skillen, "Religion and Education Policy," p. 519, n. 64, and in Coons, "Intellectual Liberty and the Schools," p. 502, nn. 20–26.

16. Compare other political systems: see McRae, *Consociational Democracy*; and Glenn, *Choice of Schools in Six Nations*.

17. Glenn, *Myth of the Common School*, pp. 63–73; see Thomas J. Curran, *Xenophobia and Immigration, 1820–1930* (Boston: Twayne, 1975).

18. Bernard J. Zylstra, "Using the Constitution to Defend Religious Rights," in Lynn R. Buzzard, ed., *Freedom and Faith: The Impact of Law on Religious Liberty* (Westchester, Ill.: Crossway Books, 1981), pp. 106–15. See also Coons, "Intellectual Liberty and the Schools"; Carl Esbeck, "Establishment Clause Limits on Governmental Interference with Religious Organizations," *Washington and Lee Law Review*, vol. 41 (1984), pp. 347–420; and idem, "Religion and a Neutral State: Imperative or Impossibility," *Cumberland Law Review*, vol. 15 (1984–85), pp. 74ff.

19. The following argument is detailed in Skillen, "Religion and Education Policy," pp. 519–29; McCarthy, Skillen, and Harper, *Disestablishment a Second Time*, pp. 124–36; McCarthy, et al., *Society, State and Schools*, pp. 169–208; and Rockne M. McCarthy, "A New Definition of 'Public' Education," in Sidey, ed., *Blackboard Fumble*, pp. 77–88.

20. See Stephen Arons, *Compelling Belief: The Culture of American Schooling* (Amherst: University of Massachusetts Press, 1986); idem, "Separation of School and State: Pierce Reconsidered," *Harvard Educational Review*, vol. 46 (1976), pp. 77–104; Coons, "Intel-

lectual Liberty and the Schools"; John E. Coons and Stephen D. Sugarman, *Education by Choice: The Case for Family Control* (Berkeley: University of California Press, 1978); Michael E. Manley-Casimir, ed., *Family Choice in Schooling* (Lexington, Mass.: Heath, 1982); Tyll van Geel, "The Search for Constitutional Limits on Governmental Authority to Inculcate Youth," *Texas Law Review,* vol. 62 (1983), pp. 199–297. For comparison with other countries, see Thomas J. La Belle, "A Comparative and International Perspective on the Prospects for Family and Community Control of Schooling," in Everhart, ed., *Public School Monopoly,* pp. 269–93; and Dennis Doyle, "Family Choice in Education: The Case of Denmark, Holland, and Australia" (National Institute of Education Contract no. EPA 30032, 1984). For a variety of views, both pro and con, on "educational choice," see the special issue of *Educational Leadership,* vol. 48 (December 1990–January 1991) on the subject.

21. For some background on the question of taxation, see Thomas W. Vitullo-Martin, "The Impact of Taxation Policy on Public and Private Schools," in Everhart, ed., *Public School Monopoly,* pp. 423–69. Recently, court and legislative battles over inequities in education funding have sprung up in Texas, Kentucky, Kansas, and other states. See "Plugging the School Tax Gap," *U.S. News and World Report* (June 25, 1990), pp. 58–59; "Big Shift in School Finance," *Time* (October 16, 1989), p. 48; David Maraniss, "Texas Schools' Financing Ruled Unconstitutional," *Washington Post* (October 3, 1989).

22. On the issue of racial discrimination, see Stephen Sugarman, "Part of the Solution Rather than Part of the Problem: A Role for American Private Elementary and Secondary Schools," *William and Mary Law Review,* vol. 31 (1990), pp. 681–93; Stephen Arons, "Educational Choice as a Civil Rights Strategy," in N. Devins, ed., *Public Values, Private Schools* (London: Falmer, 1989), pp. 63–80; Stephen Arons and Charles R. Lawrence III, "The Manipulation of Consciousness: A First Amendment Critique of Schooling," in Everhart, *Public School Monopoly,* pp. 225–68; Charles R. Lawrence III, "Segregation 'Misunderstood': The *Milliken* Decision Revisited," *University of San Francisco Law Review,* vol. 12 (Fall 1977), pp. 16–38; Coons and Sugarman, *Education by Choice,* pp. 109–24; James W. Skillen, *The Scattered Voice: Christians at Odds in the Public Square* (Grand Rapids: Zondervan, 1990), pp. 119–39, 203–5.

Conclusion

1. A few examples among the many movements for greater choice in education are the Milwaukee (Wisconsin) Parental Choice Program; voucher initiatives in California; specific legislative proposals in Minnesota, Pennsylvania, and Florida; and a movement to amend Michigan's constitution to permit wider choice among schools. For information on various reform proposals involving choice, contact the Office of Educational Research and Improvement, U.S. Department of Education, Washington, D.C. 20208-5572; Prof. John Coons, School of Law, University of California, Berkeley, CA 94720; Prof. Charles Glenn, Jr., Department of Education, Boston University, Boston, MA 02215; and Carol A. Veldman Rudie, Minnesota Federation of Citizens for Educational Freedom, 5433 Aldrich Avenue, South, Minneapolis, MN 55419. See also Lawrence Reed and Harry Hutchison, "Educational Choice for Michigan" (September 1991), a report from the Mackinac Center, 119 Ashman Street, Midland, MI 48640; and Henry Aschenbrenner, "Lessons Learned from the Educational Choice Effort in Pennsylvania" (October 1992), a report from the Pennsylvania Catholic Conference, Box 2835, Harrisburg, PA 17105.

2. Joan Biskupic, "Deaf Student's Case Sets Up Church-State Test," *The Washington Post*, February 21, 1993.

3. Ibid.

4. Joan Biskupic, "Court Reviews School Use by Church Group," *The Washington Post*, February 21, 1993.

5. The most important Supreme Court case in this regard was the 1925 *Pierce* v. *Society of Sisters*, 268 U.S. 310. See Stephen Arons, "The Separation of School and State: *Pierce* Reconsidered," *Harvard Educational Review*, vol. 46 (1976), pp. 76–104.

6. Lisa Leff, "Maryland Looks to Milwaukee for Pointers on Tuition Vouchers," *The Washington Post*, February 16, 1993.

7. See A. Polly Williams, "Inner City Kids: Why Choice Is Their Only Hope," *Imprimis* (March 1992), pp. 1–4. See also "Tough Choice," *Time* (September 16, 1991), pp. 54, 57–58.

8. Leff, "Maryland Looks to Milwaukee."

9. Dan Beyers, "Voucher Proponents Face a Formidable Foe in Maryland Teachers Union," *The Washington Post*, February 16, 1993.

10. Leff, "Maryland Looks to Milwaukee."

11. For background and comprehensive argument, see James W. Skillen, "Religion and Education Policy: Where Do We Go from Here?" *Journal of Law and Politics*, vol. 6, no. 3 (Spring 1990), pp. 503–29; Rockne M. McCarthy, James W. Skillen, and William A. Harper, *Disestablishment a Second Time: Genuine Pluralism for American Schools* (Grand Rapids: Eerdmans, 1982); Rockne M. McCarthy, et al., *Society, State, and Schools: A Case for Structural and Confessional Pluralism* (Grand Rapids: Eerdmans, 1981); John E. Coons, "Intellectual Liberty and the Schools," *Journal of Law, Ethics and Public Policy*, vol. 1 (1985), pp. 495–533; John E. Coons and Stephen D. Sugarman, *Education by Choice: The Case for Family Control* (Berkeley: University of California Press, 1978); Mary Ann Glendon and Raul F. Yanes, "Structural Free Exercise," *Michigan Law Review*, vol. 90 (December 1991), pp. 477–550; Stephen Arons, *Compelling Belief: The Culture of American Schooling* (Amherst: University of Massachusetts Press, 1986); Charles L. Glenn, Jr., *The Myth of the Common School* (Amherst: University of Massachusetts Press, 1988); Charles L. Glenn, Jr., *Choice of Schools in Six Nations* (Washington, D.C.: U.S. Department of Education, 1989). Also compare Clifford W. Cobb, *Responsive Schools, Renewed Communities* (San Francisco: ICS Press, 1992); Myron Lieberman, *Beyond Public Education* (New York: Praeger, 1986).

Index